The
Back-to-School
Book

By Suzanne Kaback, Constance Perry, and Brenda Power

SCHOLASTIC
PROFESSIONAL BOOKS

NEW YORK • TORONTO • LONDON • AUCKLAND • SYDNEY
MEXICO CITY • NEW DELHI • HONG KONG • BUENOS AIRES

Dedication

For Cathy Lewis

Cover design by Norma Ortiz
Interior design by Sarah Morrow
Cover photographs: © 2002 Steve Cole/PhotoDisc/Getty Images;
© 2002 EyeWire Collection/Getty Images
Interior photographs: S.O.D.A.; PhotoDisc/Getty Images;
EyeWire/Getty Images; Stone/Getty Images

Copyright © 2003 by Suzanne Kaback, Constance Perry, and Brenda Power
All rights reserved. Published by Scholastic Inc.
Printed in the U.S.A.
ISBN 0-439-36599-6

2 3 4 5 6 7 8 9 10   40   09 08 07 06 05 04 03

Table of Contents

Acknowledgements

Writing any book is a collaborative process, whether the authors' mentors and colleagues are near or distant. But this project was truly the effort of a team, and we are thankful for the generous gifts of wise teachers.

We thank the interns from the 2002 K-8 cohort, who worked hard during the busiest days of the launch of the school year to document so carefully the work of their mentors. These interns included Lee Birmingham, Wendy Briggs, Ellen Carr, Liz King, Sara Kreutz, Cathy LaFlamme, Jordan Main, Sue Ellen McGee, Sheri McDermott, Prescott Paine, Kat Posner, Alana Russell, and Becky Turner.

We thank the many teachers who opened up their classrooms—and, more important, their thinking—to our scrutiny, including Adele Ames, Stephen Bearor, Jennifer Becker, Kathy Bolduc, Ken Bonstein, Connie Breau, Tom Burby, Ellen Fisher, Betty Ann Haskell, Dennis Levesque, Heather Nelson, Janet Nordfors, Priscilla Sawyer, Heather Smith, Jeannie Stanhope, and Deb Yule. Special thanks to Jill Ostrow, who shared many materials from her fourth- to sixth-grade multi-age classroom.

We thank the administrators who supported this project, and have been steadfast advocates for our work throughout the past few years in Brewer, Maine, including Pam Kimball, Cathy Lewis, Bill Leithiser, and Betsy Webb.

Community begins at home, and our families sustain us. Suzy thanks Steve, Lindsay, and Will; Connie thanks Tom, Matt, and Kate; Brenda thanks Dave and Deanna.

Finally, we thank Ray Coutu, our editor. Saint Ray is the patron of all wayward authors. Thanks for nudging us to get this done over lo these many months.

Introduction

Good Beginnings

"A good beginning makes a good end." • *English Proverb*

Nothing provokes more excitement and anxiety in teachers than thoughts of the first days and weeks of school. What we do at the start of the year sets the tone for everything that will follow. There has been a flurry of books published for launching a new year with young students, emphasizing everything from room arrangement to ice-breaking activities. Information like that is so helpful, and the Internet makes it easier than ever to get it with just a few keystrokes.

But we think some of those ideas and inspirations miss a larger point: It's not what you do, but rather *how* and *why* you do it. We teachers spend so much time each summer daydreaming about our teaching—imagining what our students will be like, fussing with different room-arrangement possibilities, and fretting about how we will balance ever-increasing academic demands with the social needs of students. In this book, we share what we've learned about starting the school year with the right tone, goals, and activities for developing a vibrant community of learners that endures through the entire year. We hope you find the book rich in resources. We hope even more that you find the thinking and planning behind the ideas clear, so that you can extend and refine them throughout the entire year.

We have all been teachers for many years, working with children and fellow teachers. Our current project involves mentoring novice and veteran teachers in the Brewer School District in Maine, a site affiliated with the University of Maine. Every year, we are intrigued by teachers who have a knack for planning and launching the year with style and grace. Last year, we decided to be more systematic in observing and analyzing just what these teachers were doing. We assembled a team of pre-service interns from the University of Maine to observe them through the first days and weeks of school, and the teachers were generous in sharing the secrets of their success. We also interviewed veteran teachers throughout the country whose work we admire and compiled their advice. This book is the outgrowth of that work.

The bulk of our examples come from three very different teachers: Janet Nordfors is a fourth-grade teacher in Brewer, Maine, who has just completed her fourth year of teaching. Jill Ostrow, a veteran teacher currently residing in Maine, has worked with fourth to sixth graders in a multi-age setting. Suzy Kaback, co-author of this book, was a teacher of fifth graders for seven years before moving on to work at the University of Maine with preservice and in-service teachers. While we present examples from numerous other classrooms, ideas from these three teachers appear most frequently to give you a sense of ways new and veteran teachers approach similar issues during the first weeks of school.

Why Focus on Grades 3 to 6?

We originally planned to write a book for teachers of grades K to 8. But while observing classrooms, we quickly realized students in the upper-elementary grades have some unique needs early in the school year. This is a time of great physical, social, and emotional change for students. Their hopes and desires can be very different from those of primary-age children. A five-year-old who is new to school, for example, is often happy with any desk or storage cubby assigned to her. School is a fresh, exciting experience. But a ten-year-old already has a history, and personal space matters. His goal is to have a private space all his own, however small. A five-year-old often assumes she will succeed in school. Many ten-year-olds, however, are wary when they come to school in late summer, having experienced failure too often in the past.

The histories of older elementary students are something we can draw and build upon in the first days of school. Or we can ignore them, often with disturbing consequences—those rivalries, insecurities, and old tensions go underground, and eventually affect everything from the child's behavior on the playground to his or her performance on exams. Those histories can also reveal wonderful strengths, too—most ten-year-olds are accomplished at some task, and eager to share it with you and their peers.

In this book, we've gathered the experiences of many upper-elementary teachers who believe in the importance of building community at the start of the year. They've adopted and adapted many activities and principles from the primary grades. At the same time, they've established norms that help students prepare for changes in schedule and structure in middle school.

Building community in the upper-elementary grades involves far more than providing good ice-breaking activities. How teachers model respect for diversity and civility is critical in the first weeks of school. We also found community in the upper-elementary grades is inextricably tied to responsibility—the more responsibility teachers give students to manage the classroom and work independently, the more students thrive in their learning and relationships with each other.

The Core Ideas in This Book

As we made notes based on the observations and interviews of the preservice intern team, we were struck by five principles that seemed to be crucial to all the teachers with whom we worked:

1. Learning should be student centered.

2. Students must become independent learners.

3. Students benefit socially, emotionally, and academically when given clear expectations.

4. A safe and respectful environment is a prerequisite to learning.

5. Effective teaching is a career-long process of learning rather than a destination. It is not a set of activities, but a way of working with children.

The upper elementary teachers' different styles and approaches stem from two places: their genuine enjoyment of working with children, and their belief that each of those children is capable and important. Their caring tone is the result of their expectation and trust that students will behave, and of their avoidance of arbitrary rules. We'll show examples of how this tone can be established in the first days of school.

In his landmark study *A Place Called School* (1984), John Goodlad details observations from thousands of classrooms across the country. He found that in fourth grade, the tone and environment in classrooms became "flat"—dull, lifeless, and divorced from students' outside lives. We know from experience that the tone and environment of school doesn't have to flatten out in the upper-elementary grades. It is possible to have high academic expectations for students and still create classroom spaces that are safe, comfortable, and buzzing with learning about issues that really matter. And it all begins in the beginning, in the first days and weeks of school. We're proud to be part of the most generous profession on earth: teaching. In the following pages, we share the ideas of teachers who have given us their best advice on launching the school year. We hope you learn as much from them as we have.

Chapter 1

Before Day One

*Reaching Out to Families
and Setting Up the Classroom*

"All things are created twice.... There's a mental or first creation,

and a physical or second creation to all things."

● *Stephen R. Covey*

In *Charlotte's Web*, E.B. White offers an example of how effective words can be in changing the way people think. When Charlotte's first web appears above Wilbur's barn door, with the words "Some Pig" woven into it, Mr. Zuckerman decides that he might have misjudged the runty swine and tells his wife, "A miracle has happened and a sign has occurred here on earth, right on our farm, and we have no ordinary pig."

Mrs. Zuckerman is dubious. She says, "Well, it seems to me you're a little off. It seems to me we have no ordinary *spider*."

But Mr. Zuckerman is not dissuaded. "Oh, no," he tells his wife. "It's the pig that's unusual. It says so right there in the middle of the web." Indeed, once Charlotte names Wilbur as something special, the world begins to believe it.

There's a lesson here that can be applied to planning the school year. Your chance to name each of your students as someone special, and your class as something special, begins well before the first day. Most parents don't expect much contact from teachers in the summer, other than perhaps receiving a list of required school supplies. And, as they move up the grades, most children expect and receive less acknowledgement of their unique strengths and needs. There are small and large gestures we can make in the summer, involving reaching out to families and setting up our classrooms, that will send a message that this will be no ordinary year for our students. The process starts during the dog days of summer, as we send notes to families and begin plotting out plans for room arrangement and bulletin boards.

Reaching Out to Families

Often teachers send a brief introductory note to families in late summer, explaining expectations for the year. This section may give you ideas for going beyond such basics. Many of our suggestions don't take a great deal of time and energy, yet they have the potential to pay big dividends in building rapport with families.

Letters can be sent to parents or students. It's worth-while to do both—to send separate notes to parents and to students—so that you begin building individual relationships with both groups. We've found that kids enjoy zippy postcards with handwritten, short notes. For parents, you may want to go beyond a quick, friendly introduction, and use the first letter to start building a vision of what your classroom curriculum and community will be like. For some families, this may be the first time they have received any form of personal communication from a teacher before the school year begins.

Letters That Invite Students Into the Classroom

Fourth-grade teacher Janet Nordfors sends a letter inviting all students and their families to an open house in her classroom on an evening just before the first day of school. Her goal is to let students choose their classroom space. Janet knows that upper-elementary students cherish their privacy and growing independence. So by giving them some say over storage space, desk arrangement, and room setup, she sends a strong signal about her sensitivity to their needs. Janet arranges desks in groups of four. When students visit her classroom, she introduces herself to put names to faces, and has students try out several seats to choose one that is suitably sized and located. From there, she has them make name tags to go on their desks.

Janet also shows students and parents around the room, telling them about the different sections such as the computer center, the homework cubby section, and the current events bulletin board. She shows students where to line up when they arrive each morning and after recess, so that they will not be confused or worried on the first day.

Suzy Kaback also uses a letter to invite students into the classroom before school starts. (See sample on pages 14 and 15.) Her goal is to help them begin to feel comfortable about the space before they enter it, and to develop a sense of ownership. In her letter, Suzy invites students to join her at the end of August when she's setting up the classroom for the year. Plenty of students take her up on the invitation. They help organize books on the shelves; tape classmates' names on cubbies, desks, and coat hooks; set up the listening area; arrange art supplies; and tidy up the garden tools to use in the window garden. All of this saves Suzy time, of course, but in the process the students also get to know the terrain.

When students walk in the door on the first day of school, there is an air of confidence about them—a feeling that this is *their* room. They know where to hang their backpacks. Many of them already have school supplies loaded in their desks. And students who were not able to help set up the classroom benefit from the relaxed attitude of their peers. They sense the message that "this is our place" and can ease into the beginning of the year, just like students who did volunteer.

Like Suzy and Janet, Jill Ostrow designates a time, usually a morning, during the week before school when her multi-age fourth to sixth graders come and get to know the classroom. Because her early teaching experience was in Britain, she uses the British model of having students take far more responsibility for setting up the classroom.

When students visit in late August, the classroom walls are bare, and the desks and tables are heaped in the middle of the room. Jill has students talk about room design, help organize the furniture, and sort through books to come up with a shelving system for the classroom library.

Mrs. Kaback

Dear «student's name»,

Hello again! I'm glad we had a chance to meet on Set Up Day because now, as I write this letter, I have a clear picture of you in my mind. Luckily I have a good memory for faces! I think playing all those name games helped, too. We'll see how well you remember your new classmates' names on the first day of school, but don't worry if you've forgotten some because we have a whole year together to practice!

I hope you've had a great summer and that you're getting excited about fifth grade. I know you're going to think it's interesting, challenging, and quite comfortable now that the construction is finished at the school.

I usually send this Greetings Letter sooner than the week before school, but this summer Mr. Kaback and I traveled to Europe and didn't return until August 19. We visited two countries: Austria and Finland. In Austria, the people speak German and in Finland, they speak Finnish. I only speak English and a little French, so most of the time I was in the dark whenever I heard someone speak or tried to read a sign. Luckily, almost everyone in these countries speaks English, as well as their native language, so we survived!

I learned a few words to help me get by, such as "Guten Morgen" which means *good morning* in German and "Kiitos" (key-tows) which is *thank you* in Finnish. I also found out that in Finland, by the time most people reach ten years old, they can speak Finnish, Swedish, and English clearly. Wow!

I have plenty more stories to share about my trip and I'm looking forward to hearing about your summer. But now, I'm getting anxious to begin our school year and I'm certain you have questions about how to be ready for fifth grade.

(continued on next page)

If you're going shopping before school starts, here is a list of basic supplies. If you've already purchased supplies that don't match the list, don't worry. Just bring what you have.

1 composition notebook
(These are usually black and white with no spiral binding.)

1 three-ring binder with one-inch or bigger rings
(Trapper Keepers are not large enough to hold 5 subjects)

1 math notebook

16 pocket folders

pens and pencils

You might also want to buy colored pencils, a ruler, and scissors, although we have these in the classroom already.

That's it for supplies. I'd also like you to bring a book you're reading. If you're not reading a book right now, start thinking about the kinds of books you like to read. We can look through the classroom library to find a good one for you.

If you've had any interesting story ideas this summer, bring those with you, too. Every year I write a story that features our class on a wild adventure of some kind. This year I plan to set the story in Europe with a thrilling train scene. I got plenty of plot ideas on my trip!

By the time you receive this letter, I'll be busy getting the classroom ready for everyone. If you're looking for something to do, stop by. I'll have plenty of jobs for volunteers! Just be sure to call school first at 555-7769 to make sure I'm there.

Enjoy your last days of vacation and start looking forward to next Tuesday. I know you're going to like the "new and improved" school and have a successful fifth-grade year.

I'll see you next week!

Yours Truly,

Mrs. Kaback

Letters That Invite Family Involvement

We've also found that summer is a great time to learn about students from their families. Parents often have unusual and important information to share about their children that might be easier to share through the mail, rather than during the hectic first days of school.

When Suzy Kaback sends out the letter described above, she also sends a separate letter to parents, encouraging them to share helpful information about their children. (See sample on pages 17 and 18.) Specifically, she asks parents to write a letter telling her what she shouldn't wait to find out about their child. Her letter makes it clear that the information should be positive. Troubled home lives, past difficulties in school, and peer problems are all important factors to know at some point, but not initially. Suzy wants parents to feel comfortable bragging about their kids. She also makes it easy for them to respond by enclosing a self-addressed stamped envelope.

Responses to this request disprove the negative notions many educators have about parent involvement in the upper-elementary grades. Suzy has never received responses from less than 90 percent of parents, and what treasures their letters prove to be! (See sample on page 19.) They always provide a sneak peek into the lives of her future students and a wealth of substantive comments for each child on the very first day of school.

Suzy Kaback's Letter to Parents

SUZY KABACK

Dear «parent's name»,

I hope this letter finds you and your family healthy and enjoying the summer. I clearly remember last summer's rain and cold temperatures, so I'm thankful that we're having such a wonderful season this year.

You may be surprised to be receiving a letter from "the fifth-grade teacher," so let me explain my purpose. In a few weeks, «student's name» will find a letter of his/her own in the mailbox, but this note is just for adults. I have some news and some requests that I'd like to pass along to you.

To begin, I'm writing to let you know my plans for the fall. As many of you know, my husband Steve and I are expecting our first child at the end of October. We're thrilled, of course, but we've had to make some plans about maternity leave. For the time being, I plan to teach as long as possible. Then, when the baby is born, I'll take a few weeks off. Mr. Russell and I will be working on hiring a substitute in the early fall and I can assure you that I will look for a qualified, dedicated replacement. Please feel free to share concerns, questions, or advice(!) with me.

Thinking about becoming a mom has certainly made me more aware of the impact parents have on the lives of their children, particularly as they enter school and are turned over to the care of another person for eight hours a day. I have, however, always been a supporter of home-school communication. So, within a few weeks, you'll start receiving weekly updates about our classroom and your child's progress. It is my hope that these notes will be the basis of a year's worth of dialogue between us. We'll discuss «student's name», what's happening in class, ways you can support his/her learning at home, and ways I can extend what you do at home in school.

My hope for this kind of ongoing dialogue leads me to my first request: Would you take a few minutes to jot down some thoughts about «student's name»? I'd like your message to be positive. What shouldn't I wait to find out about him/her? What are his/her greatest strengths, proudest achievements, favorite years in school? What will I notice about «student's name»? What are the things you like or admire most about him/her?

(continued on next page)

Why am I asking you to do this? Well, I answer with another question: When a parent and a teacher communicate regularly about a child, does the child have a happier, more successful school year? On the surface it's a simple question that many people would answer with a quick "yes," but I think it deserves more deliberate consideration. A good teacher knows, however, that to make such a statement publicly takes some data. Therefore, I'd like to use any talking and writing we do throughout the year as the basis for a classroom research project that asks if there is, in fact, a connection between home-school communication and a child's school success. (Of course, all communication will be confidential, and I will request your permission for using any of our communications if opportunities arise to publish them.)

Last year I asked families to write these kinds of letters, and the results were wonderful! The only problem was that I made my request on the first day of school, and I think the letter got buried among the avalanche of other notices. Therefore, I didn't get the number of letters I'd hoped for. So, this year, I'm getting a head start on a home-school relationship, which is why you're getting this letter early!

Please write as much or as little as you'd like in the "Kid Notes." I'm just looking for that kernel of knowledge you can share with me to help start fifth grade on a confident note. I hope the self-addressed stamped envelope makes your "homework" a little easier!

And the final request: Might your soon-to-be fifth grader like to spend time helping to set up our classroom? Some would call it slave labor, but I like to think of it as volunteerism! I'll be in our room during the week prior to school and can always use help re-shelving books, hanging posters, creating bulletin boards, and so forth. If «student's name» is interested in coming to school for an hour or so one afternoon, let me know. It's a great bonding experience!

Thank you for taking the time to read this letter, and thanks in advance for responding to it. There's no rush to turn in the writing. If you don't get to it until the beginning of the school year, no problem.

Again, I wish you well and look forward to meeting you this fall.

Sincerely,

Suzy Kaback

Home Phone: 555-8420

Letter of Response From a Parent

Hi Mrs. Kaback:

Thanks for the letter. Missy would love to volunteer to help set up your room, and Nathan and I think it's a great idea. Just let us know the dates and times you need her.

Some notes about Missy:

1. She's a good friend to all.

2. She's very athletic. (She loves to dance and often choreographs her own routines.)

3. She's very dramatic—hopefully we can channel this energy in the right direction!

4. She loves to socialize—beware! This means anytime!

5. Missy struggles with school, along with self-esteem and adoption issues. Nathan and I think we need to address these issues before Missy becomes totally overwhelmed and gives up. She had a very difficult year in 4th grade. Concerns we have include:

    * She's very unorganized and needs her own personal space (she didn't have a desk last year).

    * She finds big projects overwhelming (she needs to have them broken down into smaller goals).

    * She is very distractable (she can hear minute noises and lose all concentration).

    * She gives up easily if she perceives the work is too hard.

I hope I didn't write too much. Missy is a very special girl (of course I'm her mother saying that!). She has lots of needs, but we are here to work with you. You just need to let us know. Thanks for asking us.

Phyllis Smith

Letters That Foster Responsibility in Students

Class chores are common at any grade level—even kindergartners can take responsibility for sharpening pencils, organizing books, or helping with taking attendance. By the time they reach the upper-elementary grades, students are capable of far more. Certainly, the pencils still must be sharpened and attendance taken each day. But, by third grade, students can and should take on far more important organization and classroom management tasks.

Jill Ostrow uses her back-to-school letter as a way to enlist students' help in managing and coordinating her classroom. The letter lists a series of class jobs to be carried out throughout the year. Jill organizes her students into teams that oversee these responsibilities—responsibilities that go far beyond sharpening pencils. For example, when physical education was eliminated as a separate program in her school, Jill knew she would have trouble incorporating it into the school day. So she decided to create a "recreation team." This team was responsible for developing fun, consistent physical activities for the class in lieu of a traditional class led by a P.E. teacher. (See list on pages 21 and 22.)

Students have to submit a resume and cover letter before school begins as an application for the team they want to serve on, and Jill uses this writing to help get to know students better before school began. (See instructions to students on pages 23 and 24.)

Many of these jobs merge social and academic skill building. And, because Jill sends the letter out in the summer, students get a sense before school begins that they will have far more responsibility for helping the class run well than they have had in previous years.

While Jill's plans may be far more ambitious than your own, we hope they get you thinking about new responsibilities for students and ways to prepare students for these tasks in the early days of school. When students are given real responsibility, the maturity they show to get the job done can be amazing.

Jobs, Questions, and Reflection Points
for Student Applicants

Recreational Team

Possible classmates you might work with:

Your role:

Think about types of equipment we need for our school. How much would this equipment cost us?

Think about games or activities you could teach the rest of us during a P.E. time. Think about games or activities you could organize for a recess or break time.

Theater Troupe

Possible classmates you might work with:

Your role:

Think about what you want this theater troupe to be.

If you need to practice after school, think about how kids would get home.

What are some goals you see from this troupe?

Financial Group

Possible classmates you might work with:

Your role:

We will be earning money from The Café and other fundraising activities.

You will need to find out how to open an account at the bank.

How will you keep track of our money?

How will we access the money if we need it?

Newspaper Staff

Possible classmates you might work with:

Your role:

What will the newspaper cover? How will the articles get written?

What will be in the newspaper? How often will it be published?

Community Planners

Possible classmates you might work with:

Your role:

What types of things will the community planners be doing?

How will you plan field trips for us to go on?

Community Photographers

Possible classmates you might work with:

Your role:

How will your job work? When will you take pictures?

What will happen to the pictures you take? How will we get money to develop the film?

How often do you think you will be taking pictures?

Library League

Possible classmates you might work with:

Your role:

How will your job work? How will you keep the library organized?

How will you decide upon the author of the month and design the bulletin board?

For your resume, include the following information using this outline:

Name

Address

Phone Number

Skills

This section should list all the things you think you are good at.

Education

This section should list the schools you've gone to and the years you were there.

Experience

This section should list jobs you've had in other classrooms and jobs you do around the house—anything you would consider a job-type activity.

Biographical Information

This section should include your date of birth, place of birth, and a short paragraph about where you have lived.

For your cover letter, use this form to help you organize your ideas:

Your name
Your address
The date

Jill Ostrow
Wilsonville Community School
6800 Wilsonville Road
Wilsonville, Oregon 97070

Dear Jill:

The first paragraph should let me know the team that interests you most. It should begin, "I am applying to work in the job group [name of team]."

The second paragraph should be indented and explain why you want to work in this job group and why you would be good in it.

Sign your letter, "Sincerely," with your name under it.

Surveys

Before school begins is also a great time for soliciting adult volunteers. A letter to parents might include a simple survey to complete and send back with their child. To help parents explain how they might want to help out, you might want to include questions such as the following:

- What talents, hobbies, or job skills might you be willing to share with students?

- Would you be interested in volunteering during the day to work with students? If so, please list the days and times when you are available.

- Have you volunteered in your child's classroom in the past? If so, please explain how you were involved.

Parents can also provide helpful information about their child's strengths, needs, and interests. Consider these items for your survey:

- Name a favorite book of your child's (from any point in his or her life) and describe why he or she likes it.

- What does your child do well?

- Complete the following sentences:

  My child's favorite activities are …

  If there is one thing you should know about my child, it is …

- What do you hope your child will learn this year?

Home Visits

If you're worried that families will not respond to your correspondences during the summer, don't sit and wait by the mailbox or phone. Consider making some home visits.

When Terri Austin taught sixth grade in Fairbanks, Alaska, she always made a point of visiting many families. She developed a routine that allowed her to complete visits quickly, and let families opt out of participating. We've used her methods many times and have learned a lot about students and their families in the process.

Terri sends a short letter to parents, explaining the purpose of the visits and the times and dates she will be making them. The letter also lets families know the visits will be very brief. If they would prefer not to have a visit, Terri asks them to call or send her a note. And if other plans come up, they needn't worry if they are not home.

Terri then gets out a map, sets up a route for moving quickly from house to house, and spends no more than 20 minutes at each home. In two evenings or a long Saturday, she can usually get to all families who want a visit.

We've found that seeing families on their home turf, as their guests in an environment where they are comfortable, gives us information about students we can use to build relationships all year long. Families often tell us that this is their first visit from a teacher, and they are usually touched that we take such an interest in their lives. Parents will also share important information about their own needs that they aren't able or willing to talk about in the school environment (for example, struggles with juggling daycare and homecare for their child, or concerns about his or her reading skills). Home visits aren't every teacher's cup of tea. But if you choose to make them, you can use Terri's strategies to do so efficiently.

Sample Letter for Home Visits

Dear Families:

I'm looking forward to meeting you over the coming year! Families are an important part of any classroom community, and I want to make sure you have a chance to be a part of ours.

Each summer, I like to spend a couple of evenings visiting families before the school year begins. This year, I will be making those visits on Tuesday, August 10th and Wednesday, August 11th from 4 to 8 PM. I only stop briefly at each home, and I promise I won't take more than 20 minutes of your time. My goal is to meet your family members, and answer any questions you have about the start of the school year.

These visits are optional, and you are not required to participate. If you do not want me to stop by your home for any reason, please give me a call at 555-4242. And if you have a prior commitment on August 10th or 11th and aren't home, that's fine, too. I'll just move on to the next family's house.

I will see you soon!

Ms. Power

Setting Up the Classroom

When we set up the classroom for the first weeks of school, one of our most important considerations is providing spaces for students to share information about themselves. In the upper-elementary grades, much of the responsibility for that—specifically, for creating bulletin boards and room displays, and arranging the furnishings and supplies—can be given over to students. There are many professional books and Internet sites devoted to those topics, and we'll share some of them later. But first we want to explore ways you can invite students to share their lives and histories as learners through the choices they make for bulletin boards, displays, and room arrangement.

Displays and Bulletin Boards

● "IMPORTANT ITEMS" DISPLAY

The first display Janet Nordfors sets up is a series of items that mark her life outside of school, such as a picture of her family, glass beads from her collection, her favorite books, and pictures from a trip (adapted from Kristo, 1996). Before school begins, Janet lays out the items on a table in the front of the room.

On the morning of the first day, she calls up small groups of students to look at the items for a few minutes. The importance of some of the items is fairly obvious, such as the photo of her family. But for others, it isn't. For example, few students know that Janet is an accomplished glass bead artist.

Once all students have had a chance to examine the items, they return to their seats and write down predictions about what the items mean to Janet. From there, Janet asks them to share their thoughts. She then explains that one student per week will be a VIP and have the opportunity to bring in his or her own items from home for the classmates to examine and make predictions about their significance.

● "AUTHOR OF THE MONTH" BULLETIN BOARD

Jill Ostrow creates an "Author of the Month" bulletin board in her classroom. She invariably chooses Patricia Pollaco first because, typically, Pollaco is an author students know and can enjoy by the upper elementary grades. It's hard to find a fourth or fifth grader who hasn't had at least one Pollaco story read aloud to him or her. The board invites students to share their experiences with Pollaco's work and its connections to their own lives. From there, it's easy for Jill to help students make the leap to thinking about favorite authors.

Since Pollaco is prolific, Jill also features her latest book on the board, which most likely students haven't been exposed to yet, and will probably use it as a read aloud in the early weeks of school. After creating this first "Author of the Month" board herself, Jill passes on the responsibility for selecting authors and designing the board to students, as part of the librarian job described in Chapter 1.

● "ROOM PLAN" BULLETIN BOARD

For the most part, Jill does not set up the bulletin boards or areas of the room before students arrive. Her first assignment to students is to vote on the room's set-up and create it themselves. Before school begins, Jill gets together graph paper, a sheet with the exact dimensions of the room, and a brief description of the assignment. She labels a bare bulletin board "Potential Classroom Layouts." When students arrive, they spend the first few days sketching out individual plans for the room. They then label components of their plans, post their plans on the board, and discuss them as a group. After voting on a favorite, the class brings the plan to life by arranging furnishings and materials. Jill finds that the students always come up with thoughtful and creative plans—plans that she may well have come up with herself—and they relish having some say over what the room looks like.

Items to Include on an "Author of the Month" Bulletin Board

✓ Covers of recent books

✓ A review of what you like about the author's work

✓ Sample student reviews, which are available on the Internet

✓ Comment cards in a pocket for students to write brief reviews of books

✓ A short time line or history of the author's career

✓ Excerpts from author interviews

✓ Favorite quotes from the books

Room Design

The way a room is designed says a lot about what is expected to happen there. How desks are arranged, for example, makes a powerful statement about the way a teacher expects students to learn. In Suzy Kaback's fifth-grade classroom, the desk arrangement changes frequently throughout the school year depending on the academic and social climate of the room. When collaborative projects are central to the curriculum, desks are often grouped in clusters of team members. If a guest speaker is visiting, the desks are often rearranged so that all the students are facing forward, toward the speaker. Sometimes Suzy arranges the desks into two parallel rows with pairs of students facing each other.

Diagram of Suzy Kaback's Classroom

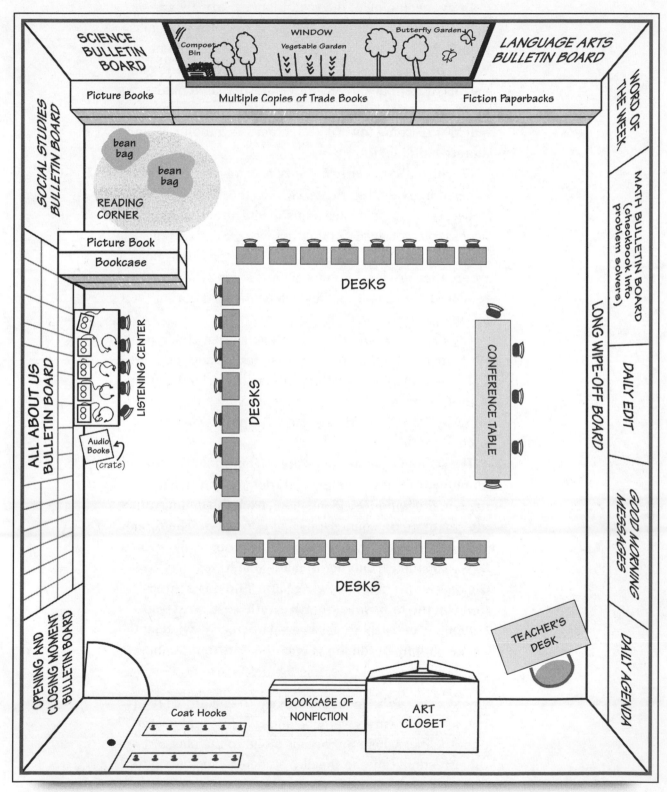

This arrangement allows for fun academic challenges, such as playing team Jeopardy, debating hot topics, and staging "talk shows" with characters from the novels the students are reading.

In the beginning of the year, though, Suzy always sets up the desks in a large horseshoe shape with students' names taped to the front of them. This arrangement works because all students can see each other (no one has his or her back to anyone) and can match names and faces easily (a way to reinforce learning names quickly). Turning toward each other is symbolic of community building, too.

Because it's too early for Suzy to know the relationships of individual students, she has the students sit in boy-girl order and makes adjustments after day one, if necessary. By the end of the first week, Suzy lets the students move their desks to a place in the horseshoe where they are most comfortable, allowing them to remain there as long as they can be focused during learning times.

Choosing a spot in the horseshoe is often challenging for students. By the time they're in fifth grade they know how distracting sitting with a good friend can be. After the first week, Suzy finds that many kids choose to sit away from their friends and wait until recess for social time.

Because first impressions are so important, Suzy does a number of things to make the room cozy. Curtains hang in the windows. Plants hang from the ceiling and are scattered on countertops and in corners. The room is loosely divided by content area with one wall devoted to social studies, another to math, one to science, and the biggest section to language arts. She posts directions on the four walls—north, south, east, west—so students can orient themselves, particularly when studying geography or thinking about the Earth's motion.

● READING CORNER

One corner of the room is designed to encourage reading. In it, there are several bean bag chairs and a large, pink recliner where Suzy reads aloud to the class. At other reading times in the day, students can sign up to sit in the recliner and on the bean bags with the understanding that no one can use the same piece of furniture two days in a row.

Bookshelves border the reading corner. While other areas' bookshelves are organized by genre, the reading corner's is generally a mishmash of new titles, with lots of picture books, multiple copies of the same book for children who want to read together, and a smattering of nonfiction including magazines, textbooks, how-to manuals, and almanacs. Suzy wants this area to feel unstructured, open for exploration.

● LISTENING AREA

Just outside the reading corner is a listening area, which contains a long, painted table, large enough for four students, with a tape recorder and earphone hub on top. In a crate on the table is a collection of audiobooks, some professionally recorded and others recorded by Suzy, alumnae of her class, and parent volunteers who like to read aloud. As often as possible, Suzy tries to have a copy of the book available with the tape so students can read along with the narrator. She includes a variety of genres and reading levels—everything from picture books and poetry collections to novels and taped recordings from Rabbit Ears radio, a production of National Public Radio and Public Radio International.

● TEACHER'S DESK/CONFERENCE TABLE

Suzy wants to create a community of learners who turn not only to her when they have questions and ideas to share, but also to each other. With this in mind, she does not situate her desk at the front of the room. Instead, it's tucked in a corner where it serves as a repository for paperwork. She does not use it for conferences. Instead, she uses a long table at the front of the horseshoe formation described earlier. In addition to conferences, reading discussions and small-group work with Suzy or other students are held there.

● BOOKCASES

Bookcases are another central feature of Suzy's room. She devotes one upright bookcase to nonfiction literature, organized by type and content: survey books, specialized books, reference books, history, science, math, art, and biography. Another whole wall of bookcases is

Ways to Organize Books in Your Classroom

You might consider arranging books by:

- First letter in the author's last name
- First letter in the title
- Genre, fiction and nonfiction
- Content area
- Awards they've won
- Text set (i.e., groups of books from a variety of genres that cover a single topic)

You might also consider special sections within larger sections, such as:

- Writer's craft (Books that show good examples of leads, use of verbs, effective characterizations, strong dialogue, enticing chapter titles. Finding and organizing these books might be an ongoing project that students contribute to throughout the year.)

- Reading strategies (Books that support questioning, predicting, inferencing, connecting, retelling, and visualizing. This could be another ongoing project for students to work on.)

At the end of the day, when students are cleaning up the room, they should use classification skills to get the job done. Of course, those skills also make locating and reshelving books easier, too.

filled with fiction, organized loosely by author. Suzy finds that having a system is a good way to teach her students the usefulness of being organized.

Predictability can be comforting to students. For that reason, Suzy has places in the room that never change. For example, every morning she posts the daily agenda on the wipe-off board in a permanent spot. She also writes a welcome message to the class every day that contains interesting news, reminders, and often a task she expects them to complete before the opening of the day, such as:

- Read the sentence written below and find the misspelling/grammatical error.

- Find the basket of new books from the book order and choose one that looks interesting. Be prepared to share it with the class.

- Clean your desk.

- Read the new poem posted in the poetry corner.

- Brainstorm everything you know about _____. (Fill in the blank with a curricular area you plan to introduce that day—The Civil War, mollusks, fractions, Canada … whatever.

- Solve the math problem below.

- Look up the definition of this week's Word of the Week.

Desk arrangement, book displays, the conference table, the listening center, the reading corner, and decorative flourishes that lend comfort are Suzy's priorities when she designs her classroom at the start of the year. She deliberately leaves most bulletin boards empty, except for a covering of colorful paper, in preparation to display student work. She keeps a folder of decorative materials to highlight children's work, but enlists students to use them only to embellish borders in ways they find meaningful. There are always students who finish work early or who have trouble focusing. They are excellent candidates for bulletin board work.

Closing Thoughts

We began this chapter with a metaphor from *Charlotte's Web* about how words and actions can change the way people think. E.B. White, the book's author, loved using the image of spiders weaving webs in his writing. It's a powerful image—those nearly invisible strands so carefully woven together in a structure planned from the start. The notes, gatherings, and visits made before the school year begins can form strands like those—strands that connect you to your students and their families, the start of your community. And your careful arrangement of desks, book displays, and bulletin boards marks your first moments of thinking through who is a part of your classroom, and what you want that community to be.

In our own work, we are surprised at how often we return to a nugget of information about a student gleaned from a visit to her home, or an insight about a child's passions first revealed on a parent survey, or inspiration for curriculum that came during a chat with students while setting up a bulletin board in mid-August. Time getting to know students and families as you roll up your sleeves in preparation is time well spent.

Chapter 2

Day One

*Getting to Know One Another
and Establishing Routines*

"We need to take the time, no matter how hectic our days become,
to stare out at the sea or to sit quietly in the yard or up on
the rooftop and ask ourselves what it is we care about and
how honestly we share our concerns, hopes, and passions
with one another and our students. New methods of
instruction and evaluation will continue to evolve in direct
proportion to who we are, and how much of that we are willing to bring into our teaching." ● *Maureen Barbieri*

There are many wonderful ways to plan the first day and
activities that are sure to delight students in the upper-

elementary grades. But we've found what matters most is the thinking behind any plan—the connections we make between a far-reaching vision of what we want our classrooms to be and the first steps in reaching that vision. Setting a tone on that first day, one that invites questions about and engagement with the curriculum and one another, is no small task.

In this chapter, we take you into the mind of one teacher, Suzy Kaback, a co-author of this book who has taught fifth grade for many years. We think you'll pick up many ideas for how to organize the day and get to know your students as you read Suzy's description of her typical first day. But we hope her thinking, her explanations of the long-term goal behind each activity, serves as a catalyst for your own thinking. We hope it helps you mull over how you can make your own first day a unique experience for yourself and your students.

Big Hopes and Bad Dreams:
One Teacher's First Day

Suzy is always relieved when the first day of a new school year arrives. Before the first day, her sleep is fraught with nightmares featuring a classroom of unruly students who throw things at each other and at her, and who do not listen to her strangled cries for order. The nightmares always end with the shadow of her principal filling the doorway. He watches from the hallway, aghast at this spectacle of her failure as a teacher. Suzy knows she's not alone. Ask any teacher about her dreams before the first day and you'll be entertained by the agony they evoke.

Years of experience, however, have proven that no first day is ever as devastating as what happens in Suzy's nightmares. That said, there's no guarantee of success on her first day. Success results from careful planning with an eye toward what will make a new group of students feel comfortable and confident. As described in the previous chapter, Suzy's preparations for the first day begin weeks before students come through the door. She wants her students to feel ownership of their space right away. By asking them to help dust, scrub, set up desks, and design bulletin boards, all while talking naturally with each other and with her, she starts them on their way to calling the room their own.

But Suzy also spends many hours alone planning the structure of the opening day. As she plans, she frequently self-checks her ideas. She doesn't want a day filled with "cutesy" exercises that are fun for five minutes but have no lasting value. She strives to design activities that have a life after the first day, activities that become part of the class's daily routine because they're built on the foundation of learning and community building.

Over the years, Suzy has developed some practical ideas for creating a community that will sustain the class throughout the year. These ideas fit with her understanding of upper-elementary students' need to have a space of their own, to have opportunities to showcase their interests and talents, and to take risks in a supportive environment. And she demonstrates her commitment to and understanding of students by putting herself "out there" on day one. If she asks students to try something new and to feel safe doing it, then it's only fair that she take risks and expect the group's support when she does.

First Bell: Making Everyone Feel Welcome

As students file into the classroom on the first day, Suzy stations herself at the door and greets them individually. She usually knows most of the kids already, thanks to the late-summer get-the-room-ready sessions described on page 13. Being able to call a student by name from the moment he walks in on the first day is powerful. It shows that Suzy cares enough to remember him and knows he belongs there. At the same time, Suzy recognizes that not all students are able to make it to the late-summer sessions. Some were still on vacation, some are last-minute transfers, some couldn't find a way in, and some had no interest in starting school a single second before they had to. So, while Suzy nurtures those relationships that have been established, she's careful to avoid making anyone feel like an outsider. When she sees a student she doesn't recognize, she finds out her name then asks a student who helped label desks and coat hooks to direct the student to her spaces. That way, the child sees right away that the teacher isn't the only one who cares to know who she is; peers have been expecting her, too, and know she belongs with them.

On each desk, Suzy places a marbled composition notebook and a fun pen. It's exciting for the kids to receive this gift, which not only delights but also suggests how important writing will be throughout the year. Suzy gives students composition notebooks because pages can't be ripped out easily. (They're sewn in, rather than attached by a spiral binding.) Students use the notebooks as an idea place. Suzy doesn't evaluate entries, but she offers to read students' ideas, works in progress, musings, clippings, mentor poems—any writing on which they may want feedback. Students use these notebooks on the first day during writing workshop, which is described below.

Once everyone is seated, Suzy welcomes students and tells them that their first day will be filled with movement, questions, and explanations—lots of explanations. She explains that they will begin some routines that will be repeated almost daily, until the final day of school in June. These routines include the opening and closing moments, the daily agenda, read-aloud time, and many expectations for behaviors that support community building.

Opening Moment: Spotlight on a Class Star

Jeff Wilhelm, our colleague at the University of Maine, always begins each class with an opening moment. Actually, he doesn't begin the class; his students do. An opening moment is an opportunity for a student to share with the class something of interest. When Suzy learned about this idea, she immediately implemented it—and with great success. In her experience with opening moments, students have done magic tricks, read a favorite poem, taught the class how to tie a knot, shared a piece of their writing, displayed souvenirs from a vacation, sung songs, led the class in a yoga exercise, and led a book talk about a recommended title. The list is long and varied. One of Suzy's favorite opening moments, though, was the day a student brought in a box full of bubble wrap, spread it out on the floor of the classroom, and invited the class to relieve some stress by jumping around until the bubbles were all popped.

On the first day, Suzy demonstrates an opening moment with a curricular connection. The result is two-fold. Students see how to execute one kind of opening moment while also receiving a subtle introduction to a content area. For example, one year her class was to study Native Americans in social studies, so Suzy used the first opening moment to show how to do Indian beading on a loom. After her demonstration, she gave each student a wooden loom, made by a generous industrial arts teacher, and explained that in the coming weeks the class would learn how to craft a piece of Native American jewelry. During the first month of school, she held craft workshops a few times a week when the students would work on their looms. By the time their parent night arrived, her students had created a museum-quality display of Native American jewelry created by the class artisans.

This activity had true lasting value. Although Suzy only dedicated a few weeks to the workshops, some students continued beading until the last day of school.

Possible Opening Moments

Possible Opening Moments

✔ Do a magic trick

✔ Tell a joke

✔ Share a collection (rocks, marbles, books, bean bag dolls)

✔ Teach the class a song

✔ Read a poem

✔ Demonstrate a craft or skill such as tying knots, playing marbles or jacks, performing jump-rope rhymes, doing a karate move, or making a friendship bracelet

✔ Show pictures from a favorite vacation

✔ Host a tea party

✔ Have a quiet interlude; play music while the class rests or draws

✔ Teach a yoga posture

Not all opening moments have this kind of longevity, but they all nurture community and learning to some extent. And, of course, most teachers don't have a loom for every student, nor do most share Suzy's passion for crafting jewelry. But there are many other ideas for opening moments that can serve a similar purpose—to bring hands-on learning into the room in the first moments of school. (See sidebar, left.)

First Agenda: Getting a Feel for the Day

After an energizing opening moment, Suzy focuses students on their daily agenda. She has found that older kids appreciate knowing where the day is taking them, so she tells them. But she's also careful to stress that plans can change. Flexibility is important to building a successful community, yet older children will quickly adapt to routines and become dependent on them. For that reason, Suzy offers a daily schedule that's predictable but loose. Her goal is to create students who don't melt down with a small schedule change, such as when writing workshop takes longer than expected and causes the poetry reading to be moved to the next day.

Each morning before the class arrives, Suzy organizes her thinking by writing the plan for the day on one side of the wipe-off board at the front of the class. She lists the order of events for the day, including those happening in the classroom as well as those outside—specials, lunch, recess, and so forth. Eventually, Suzy turns over responsibility for writing the agenda to the students. A volunteer writes the regular academic periods for the day, and Suzy adds any marquee events, such as a guest speaker, field trip, or the beginning of a new project. She avoids assigning time ranges to each period because students tend to watch the clock too closely. This allows her to extend a successful science lab, for example, without students reminding her that it's 10:30 and time to move on to math.

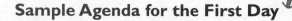

Sample Agenda for the First Day

- Greet students at the door. Use names as often as possible. Enlist kids to help each other get settled. Have a composition notebook and pen on each student's desk.

- Demonstrate an Opening Moment.

- Post a daily agenda and talk about it with the class.

- Play a name game, such as "I Wonder If …"

- Have a healthy snack, something special just for the group.

- Allow an extra long recess and make yourself visible to each of your students during the break.

- Tour the school, armed with a list of student-generated questions about the building. Arrange to have specialists, the principal, and support staff waiting to introduce themselves.

- Eat lunch in the cafeteria with the students.

- Read aloud. Choose a book that sparkles with humor from page one.

- Begin writing workshop. Prepare to share the first installment of your "Class Story." Post a list of fun first-day writing ideas to prompt kids who might have trouble getting started during independent writing time.

- Introduce the All About Us board.

- Play another name game.

- Demonstrate a Closing Moment. Recite "Big Fat Hen."

Getting students oriented to the agenda takes time. Suzy spends several weeks fielding students' questions that often can be answered by reading the daily agenda ("Do we have P.E. today?" "When is writing

**Web Sites With
Other Name Games**

http://www.education-
world.com/a_lesson/
lesson019.shtml

http://www.atozteacher
stuff.com/lessons/Backto
SchoolActivities.shtml

http://www.col-ed.org/
cur/misc/misc04.txt

http://teachers.net/
lessons/posts/164.html

time going to be?"). Eventually, though, students start
checking the board, and she no longer needs to
answer such logistical questions. By October students
know that, after they have unpacked and found their
seats, they are expected to read the agenda and inter-
nalize their day.

Introductory Name Game: "I Wonder If ..."

Nothing says, "I know you!" more powerfully than
calling someone by his or her first name. Suzy plans
two blocks of time for Name Games on the first day
of school—one at the beginning of the day and one at
the end—to help students learn each other's names
quickly. Some of her ideas come from her work at an
adventure-based learning program, where knowing
each other's names was not only polite, but also
imperative. When a kid was hanging 50 feet up on
a rock-climbing wall and refused to move another
inch, "Hey you, you can do it. We know you can!"
didn't have the same impact as, "Okay, Sarah, let's
talk you down."

In the classroom, learning names isn't tied to safety,
but it does have a substantial affective impact. The
first game Suzy's class plays—"I Wonder If ..."—gives
an opportunity for students to learn not only each
other's names, but also interesting facts about each
other. Suzy has students form a circle of chairs in the
middle of the horseshoe of desks. She begins by
standing in the middle of circle and saying, "Hi, my
name is Mrs. Kaback." And the class is instructed to
respond by saying, "Hi, Mrs. Kaback" in unison. Then
she announces, "I wonder if ..." and chooses an ending such as "... anyone has ever been out of the state
of Maine." Students who have traveled outside the
state stand up, and Suzy selects one of them to
replace her in the center of the circle. This student
then introduces herself and offers her own "I wonder
if ..." statement, and the game continues.

"I Wonder If . . ." Prompts

I wonder if anyone:

- has ever read a Harry Potter book.

- is allergic to peanuts.

- thinks math is the best subject in the world.

- walks to school.

- has twins in their family.

- has ever been on an airplane.

- is really good at spelling.

- plans to play soccer on the team this year.

- watches *Cyberchase* on PBS.

- is nervous about what fifth grade is going to be like.

"I Wonder If ..." is not competitive. In fact, it's quite social because students choose prompts to learn particular information about their classmates. The group learns a lot about the person in the middle, too. For example, if that person asks, "I wonder if anyone has ever reached level 44" in a favorite Nintendo game, the class can be pretty certain that she's a fan of the game. "I Wonder If ..." is an effective way to learn each other's names while finding common threads that bring the class together as a community.

First Snack: Good Nutrition for Powerful Learning

Kids and food are a winning combination. During her class's first snack time, Suzy talks about the importance of eating healthy food and its effect on learning. In his book *Teaching with the Brain in Mind* (1998), Eric Jensen cites compelling research that documents the role of nutrition in learning. "Food must supply the nutrients necessary for learning, and the critical nutrients include proteins, unsaturated fats, vegetables, complex carbohydrates, and sugars." As teachers, we have a responsibility to support families in building healthy eating habits because, as Jensen notes, "Most kids eat to get rid of their hunger and lack sufficient information to eat for optimal learning." Jensen also points out the importance of water, stating, "Dehydration is a common problem that's linked to poor learning." Suzy makes sure her students have access to water throughout the day, encouraging them to bring water bottles to keep on their desks.

To promote healthy eating habits at snack time, Suzy brings in a platter of cold watermelon slices on the first day and tells students that this fruit is her favorite food. That way, the class learns something else about her and gets some healthy nourishment.

Sources of Information on Healthy Eating Habits and Snack Ideas

Teaching with the Brain in Mind, Eric Jensen (Association for Supervision and Curriculum Development)

Comprehensive School Health, Linda Meeks and Philip Heit, editors (Meeks Heit Publishing Company)

Consider sending home a list of Web sites with healthy snack recipes!

http://www.yumyum.com (Click on "kids")

http://family.go.com/recipes/kids

http://www.ecsu.ctstateu.edu/depts/edu/textbooks/healthyeating.html

http://www.healthyfridge.org/kidsrec.html

(The unintended result is that, for every special occasion throughout the year, Suzy is inundated with watermelon-themed gifts: magnets, earrings, candles, potholders, candy, and so forth.) In Suzy's school, classroom teachers are responsible for health instruction, and snack time is a perfect springboard for introducing all kinds of ideas about healthy eating habits. Something as seemingly simple as the first snack offers a significant opportunity for linking community goals (eating together is a cultural experience) with curricular requirements (making wise food choices to support a healthy lifestyle).

First Recess: The Class Breaks Out

By midmorning, the students are clamoring to race around a playground and debrief their classmates about the new school year. Suzy always offers an extra long recess on the first day. Before students head out, though, she talks to them about expectations, including the school rules governing recess time and why the rules are important.

While students play and talk, Suzy makes herself very visible because she knows that recess is a great time to learn more about the needs and interests of students. She watches a group playing kickball, eavesdrops on a conversation that doesn't seem to be private, checks in with the kid who's hanging out alone by the fence, pushes a couple of kids on the swings. By actively touring the playground, Suzy communicates her curiosity about their lives and interests beyond the classroom.

This is a great habit to continue all year long, but it's especially important in the first weeks. Older kids appreciate being acknowledged for their excellent quarterbacking skills, for their extensive collection of colored stones, for the 10 friendship bracelets they can produce in a 20-minute recess. And spending five minutes with those universal fringe kids, the ones who seem to spend all their free time alone, often gives them the psychological boost they need to feel confident. Suzy tries not to get too involved in students' social affairs outside the classroom, but she makes it known that she's aware of where they are and what they like to do.

School Tour: Getting Used to the Geography

A tour of the school is an important first-day event. Even if students are entering their fifth year in the same school building, it's useful to take a walk around and talk about improvements made over the summer, new classroom assignments, new teachers, eye-catching bulletin boards. Veteran students can be welcome guides for classmates who are new to the school. It's especially important for all students, especially those who are new, to get an overview early so that when they leave the comfortable confines of their classroom, they feel confident that they'll find their way back.

Suzy always begins her tour by distributing a jazzy map of the building's layout and inviting questions. Then, armed with the map and questions, she and the students take a trip around the school. She arranges to have specialists, the principal, and support staff waiting to introduce themselves.

Some years, after its tour, Suzy's class goes on a scavenger hunt. She has students choose a partner, gives them a list of items to obtain, and sends them off with instructions to be absolutely silent during their hunt. Items might include the signature of the P.E. teacher; an art supply; a drawing of the cafeteria's layout; the most recent trophy earned by a school team; and a count of the number of lockers in the north wing, exits in the building, or classrooms in the building. This provides another opportunity for more experienced kids to work with newcomers in accomplishing a challenging task. By the time they've finished the tour and the scavenger hunt, most students report feeling less anxious about getting around.

First Read Aloud: Wise Choices for Riveting Reading

After the first lunch of the new school year—during which Suzy tries to make herself as available as possible—and a second recess, the class returns to the room for a treasured part of the day: read-aloud time. Suzy tells students that the half hour she reads to them is sacred time. They move into the reading corner. Suzy always sits in her 20-year-old pink recliner, which was handed down to her by her grandmother. The students gather at her feet, sitting, sprawled on their stomachs or backs, wedged close together, or set apart, as comfortable as possible. If they want to draw or doodle while they listen, she allows it as long as it's not distracting. Girls often bring accessories to "do" each other's hair, hitched in a line like locomotive cars. Suzy allows students to be near anyone they choose, with the understanding that talking is not allowed. Some teachers don't allow children to draw or sit close enough to touch, but Suzy

Read Aloud Ground Rules

1. Please listen during the read aloud. Talking is prohibited.

2. You may sit with whomever you choose, keeping in mind rule #1. You may also choose where you'd like to sit, but please stay within the established boundaries.

3. You may doodle or write during read aloud as long as it does not distract you or a neighbor from listening.

4. If we have multiple copies of the book being read, you may read along.

5. Keep a comfortable distance from those around you.

Great First-Day Read Alouds

Poppy by Avi (Camelot)

Bingo Brown and the Language of Love by Betsy Byars (and sequels) (Puffin)

The Watsons Go to Birmingham by Christopher Paul Curtis (Bantam Books)

Nothing's Fair in Fifth Grade by Barbara Declements (Puffin)

The Great Brain by John Fitzgerald (and sequels) (Yearling Books)

The Worst (Best) School Year Ever by Barbara Parks (HarperTrophy)

Soup by Robert Peck (and sequels) (Random House)

finds these behaviors build intimacy and help students feel relaxed, which benefits the classroom community. The fact that she usually only has to explain these ground rules once shows how much students appreciate the down time during a busy day. They settle into the read-aloud routine gratefully.

Suzy is deliberate about the book she chooses for her first read aloud. She likes to begin with one that contains humor, avoids heavy messages, and features kids who are like the fifth graders she teaches. If her students connect with the characters and are entertained by the plot, Suzy's first read aloud will be a success.

First Writing Period

Reading and writing are the bedrock on which Suzy builds the learning in her classroom. Therefore, in addition to reading aloud, doing some writing on the first day together is important. Rather than talking about the structure and rules of writing workshop, though, Suzy spends the first writing period sharing her own writing and giving students time to compose a bit on their own.

Collaborative publishing is an effective way to encourage community. When students create a book that includes pieces by everyone, they become a team with a tangible product to show for it. One interesting way Suzy shows students how unifying writing can be is by composing a class adventure story, which started as a writing experiment years back and proved to be a huge hit with the kids.

Class stories usually have five or six chapters. Suzy reads aloud one each week during the first month of school. Their plots vary from year to year, based on students' personalities, world events, and school activities, but the basic premise is the same: Suzy's class is in trouble and has to find a way out. One year the story involved an evil bus driver who kidnapped the class for ransom during a field trip. Another year, a giant alien spaceship abducted the class while it was outside at recess. And another year, a student fell under the spell of a wizard, and Suzy's class had to rescue her. The goal of the story is to write about the class in a way that suggests camaraderie and playfulness, qualities Suzy hopes the class will embrace in real life. In other words, if she writes about the students being close and supportive of each other, they'll come to believe it themselves and act on it.

The chapter she shares on the first day introduces the story's problem and ends with a cliffhanger. While the chapter talks about the group as a whole, Suzy is careful to write about individual students at least once in subsequent chapters, attributing witty dialogue to the class clown, allowing the class "techie" to save the day by breaking a difficult computer code, having the athlete use her abilities to outrun the

The Perfect Day
Chapter 4

The ride to the airport seemed to take seconds, even though I knew the trip was twenty minutes in a normal car. By the time we pulled into the terminal, everyone had finished a perfect breakfast and the driver was explaining our next event.

"Your plane leaves at 8:35. It is now 8:15, but you have plenty of time to board. You will fly directly to Puerto Vallarta, Mexico. Your flight should be less than five hours. From there you'll take a luxury bus to Chichen Itza and the Mayan ruins."

Some kids were eyeing the arriving and departing planes nervously. Many people had never flown before and were not prepared for the experience.

"Hey, flying is no problem," Tessie reassured us. She could tell by the anxious vibes that some people needed to be calmed down.

"It's a lot like being on a bus, except that you're in the air. You just sit in the seat, put on the safety belt, and lie back. The flight attendant will bring you as much soda as you can drink."

Her explanation seemed to relax the group and everyone piled out of the limo when it stopped by the terminal.

"Where do we go?" I asked.

"Just follow the signs that say 'Kaback Party'" the driver informed me.

I looked around and quickly saw the colorful signs and pointing arrows with my name on them.

"This way everyone!"

"Mrs. Kaback, is it true we see movies during the flight?" Dan asked.

"Well, this is a long flight, so I expect we will see a movie. Any preferences?"

"How about Jurrasic Park? I've never seen prehistoric creatures in flight. Get it? IN FLIGHT?" Dan began laughing hysterically at his own joke.

"What about pteradactyls?" Evan asked teasingly.

"Very funny," Dan answered, not pleased with Evan's sense

A page from one of Suzy's class stories. Whenever possible, she weaves in topics related to content-area studies. In this story, for example, she has her students visit Chichen Itza to tie in with their study of Mayan culture.

villain and deliver the magic antidote safely. Students love these stories and wait anxiously for each installment. It takes a lot of time to write the stories, so even though the class clamors for sequels, Suzy only writes one a year.

After sharing her chapter, Suzy invites the class to write. Typically students are so entertained by her story that they need little encouragement to jump in. Although she offers suggestions for first-day writing, students often come with ideas because of the letter Suzy sends out in late summer. (See pages 17 and 18.) Many students choose to write a class story themselves, although they usually feature the writer's closest friends rather than the whole class.

Suzy attributes the success of the first writing period to the power of example. Writing with and for her class demonstrates how much Suzy values the process of writing. It lets students know that she faces the same joys and struggles they do. When her students see that she writes, they know it's a genuine activity, not a filler that keeps them at their desks.

The class story also gives Suzy plenty of material to use in writing workshop. She plans mini-lessons around each week's chapter. After reading one aloud, she often puts sections on the overhead to demonstrate a skill or craft technique. The class talks about characterization, dialogue, leads, chapter titles, strong verbs, and plot development in a context that is entertaining and relevant.

The final test of the class story's appeal usually comes in the end of September, during parent night. Students clamor for the binder that holds the story and show it to their parents, quickly flipping to the page on which they appear.

By featuring the class in a story, Suzy helps her students learn about each other, fostering camaraderie in an unusual context. After all, it takes teamwork to defeat the evil forces that threaten their well-being. Students might as well stick together in case of future trouble.

Prompts for First-Day Writing

- Describe your perfect day if money and time were no objects.

- Imagine you won a contest to design your dream bedroom. Describe your design.

- If you were going to live on a deserted island and you could take one person, one book, and one object of your choice, who and what would you take? Explain why.

- Imagine you're having dinner at your favorite restaurant with a person of your choice, living or dead, famous or not. Where are you eating and who's your companion? Write down the dinner-time conversation between the two of you.

- What do you want to be when you grow up and why?

- Is it better to be a boy or a girl? Explain your answer.

All About Us Bulletin Board

Starting an All About Us bulletin board is a first-day activity that supports all-year community building. To prepare, Suzy uses yarn to divide her largest bulletin board into as many squares as there are students in the class. She also creates a square for herself, as well as a few extras for new students and/or a student teacher who might arrive later. Each student is assigned a square to decorate with objects that will help the class learn more about him or her.

On the first day, Suzy shows students what they might include in their squares. She has photographs of her family, a small earring in the shape of a watermelon, some coins from European countries she's visited, a poem by Milton, and a ticket stub from the Broadway show *Rent*. She shares the items with the students and attaches them to the board, using push pins and plastic bags to store fragile or solid items. Each morning after the first day, several students take a couple of minutes to talk about their items and post them in their squares. It takes about a week for everyone to have a turn, so each day the board grows more colorful and intriguing.

All About Us Bulletin Board

The All About Us board celebrates each student's individuality, but it also reveals how interesting that class is as a group. The board is well known around school. Teachers, the principal, and former students always take time to pop in and see what the current class has designed. The board is a favorite at the fall open house, too, when parents are treated to a gallery viewing of what makes the class special.

The Many Uses of the All About Us Bulletin Board

As the year goes on, the All About Us board evolves to meet the changing class identity. It is a wonderful community builder that grows throughout the year.

Toward the Beginning of the Year...

Personal Belongings

During the first weeks of school, invite students to fill in their assigned squares with items that reveal things about them. Why wait to find out about their interests and personalities?

Homemade Turkeys

For Thanksgiving, try this family project: Cut out large oaktag turkeys and ask students to decorate them with their families, using a variety of materials.

In Suzy's classroom, turkeys have been decorated with seeds, spices, feathers, and layers of beautiful paper (foil, tissue paper, origami paper). Turkeys have arrived covered with everything from family pictures to newspaper comics to uncooked pasta. The have been illustrated by hand using paint, crayons, oils, and markers. They have been "quilted" with scraps of clothing from each family member (for example, from the baby's spit-up cloth, dad's cooking apron, grandma's Easter hat, a favorite holey tee shirt). Each year Suzy decorates a turkey to hang in her square, which serves as a model. She shares stories of past years' turkeys, too, highlighting the project's emphasis on family participation.

Start talking about the project just after Halloween so families have time to plan and prepare their turkeys for display before the Thanksgiving vacation.

Holiday Motifs

At Christmas/Hannukah/Kwanzaa time, ask students to decorate their square with a winter holiday theme. Give them construction paper, wrapping paper, old holiday cards, pipe cleaners, beads, string, colored paint, glue, sequins, glitter, and other craft supplies to decorate a custom-size piece of paper that will then hang in their square.

Mailboxes

At mid-year, clear off the All About Us board to create a wall of mailboxes. Invite students to use their squares to pass notes to each other (written during sanctioned times, of course). Push pins allow kids to stick notes in the appropriate spot.

For the first few weeks of this phase, Suzy makes sure each child gets a piece of mail from her at least once each week. Sometimes she posts a funny joke in a student's box, a clipping from the newspaper related to his or her particular interest, a note telling a child that she enjoyed his or her opening moment that week, or a sheet of stickers to use on his or her notebooks. Students e-mail each other constantly, but she doesn't want them to lose the joy of traditional letter writing. Everyone loves receiving "real" mail as much as virtual mail.

Another way Suzy encourages written communication around the room is by giving everyone three construction-paper stars at the beginning of the week. She asks students to distribute the stars throughout the week to three classmates who deserve recognition for a kind act. On the star, they write why they are awarding it. For example, "You helped Kyra pick up her books after her backpack fell," or "I saw you let Mrs. Kaback cut in front of you in the lunch line so she could have longer to eat yesterday." These little "points of praise" are excellent community builders because everyone tries to catch someone being helpful or considerate. Students look forward to finding stuff in their boxes, and, since sixty or more stars circulate a week, everyone is guaranteed to get at least one in that time.

Content-Area Projects

Display content-area projects in each square. For example, in science, when Suzy's students were studying the anatomy of a flower, they dissected different blooms, glued each anatomical part on a piece of black construction paper, and labeled each section. The students then posted their "autopsies" in their squares. The class also diagrammed worms, fish, hearts, reproductive systems, and cells and put them in their squares. When students finished pieces of writing that made them especially proud, they posted them. Illustrations of famous people from history or diagrams of battle sites were also hung in students' squares. Some students posted challenging math problems, tongue twisters, jokes, or riddles. The expectation to post work often inspired students to put more effort into their finished projects, and the variety of work on display added vibrancy to the room.

Propaganda Displays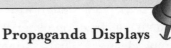

Suzy's students study propaganda in advertising and then try to create advertisements for a healthy food, using the techniques of professional ad writers. When their ads are posted in the All About Us squares, the class has quite a billboard supporting healthy eating habits.

Person of the Week

Keep a couple of spaces free in the All About Us board for visitors and newcomers. Each year, Suzy usually has at least one student teacher. She also usually welcomes a new child into the class community, and one of his or her first jobs is to tell the class about himself or herself, using the assigned square.

The class also has a featured Person of the Week from the school's faculty or staff who is invited to share his or her interests by filling in a designated square. Everyone learns fascinating facts about the principal, the cafeteria workers, the school's administrative assistant, the nurse, guidance counselor, and select teachers from other grade levels and curricular areas. Last year the class chose twelve people to feature, which allowed each one to display his or her work for two weeks. (One year the principal asked for a permanent space and joined the class for each new phase of the board, from turkey decorating to mail service and propaganda posters!)

Toward the End of the Year...

Tributes

Students use squares in more personal ways to write tributes to classmates who have been important during the year. Some students choose to write about several friends, others about only one. Some post photographs as well. Suzy also asks that each student choose a favorite poem to dedicate to at least one of their classmates, allowing her to integrate their year-long study of poetry with the affective goals of the tribute project. Students design their tributes on pieces of oaktag that are cut to fit the squares on the board. On the last day of school, students can deliver their tributes to the featured person or take them home for posterity.

Closing Name Game: Remember Me

By the end of the first day, students are more comfortable with each other. They've had plenty of opportunities to interact and, as a result, they know many of their classmates' names. Playing a second name game shows them how far they've come as a group in a single day.

One activity Suzy's fifth graders enjoy is called Remember Me. Again, they circle their chairs inside the horseshoe of desks. Suzy asks for a volunteer and then has that student say her name and add an adjective that both begins with the same letter of her first name and reveals something about her personality. For example, Sarah might say, "I'm Sleepy Sarah because my parents can never wake me up on school mornings."

The next child is charged with reciting the previous child's "nickname," and then coming up with his own: "She's Sleepy Sarah and I'm Nimble Nick because I can climb trees like a monkey." Hannah, who follows Sarah and Nick, would say, "There's Sleepy Sarah and Nimble Nick, and I'm Hungry Hannah because I can never get enough to eat." The game is most challenging, of course, for the final players, but the use of alliterative adjectives usually helps their memory.

Suzy writes down everyone's nickname during Remember Me. On the last day of the year, she pulls out the list and reads it to the class. It's always entertaining to see who has lived up to his name and who hasn't.

Closing Moment: A Challenge

Like the opening moment, the closing moment is a ritual Suzy and her class continue throughout the year. It's an opportunity for them to come together as a group and enjoy a presentation by a member of their classroom community before saying goodbye for the day.

Suzy models the year's first closing moment to give students a sense of how it's done. From there, students take over responsibility. The idea for her most successful first closing moment came one summer when she was visiting her father-in-law, a man who loves to play with language. He taught Suzy's son a crazy poem called "Big Fat Hen," which he learned at summer camp. Suzy thought the poem was catchy, so she memorized it and uses it as her closing moment on the first day.

Suzy introduces "Big Fat Hen" by distributing a photocopy of it to each student and hangs an enlarged version on the language bulletin board. Suzy then explains that anyone who memorizes the poem and performs it, at any time during the school year, will earn an extra ten minutes of recess for the whole class.

On mornings when a student announces that he or she is going to try to recite "Big Fat Hen," the whole class snaps to attention—and is always impressed by and appreciative of a successful performance. (It doesn't take long for someone to figure out that

I Got A Big Fat Hen!

I got a big fat hen

A couple of ducks

Three brown bears

Four running hares

Five fat foxes

Six slimy salamanders

Seven silly Siamese sailors sailing the seven seas

Eight egotistical elephants

Nine nimble nitwits nonchalantly nibbling gnats

Ten typical topographers translating type on top of a tent

Eleven elegant elves elevated to the eleventh elf

Twelve traveling travelers trumpeting twenty-two triumphant trumpets triumphantly

Thirteen thriving thieves thieving thirty-three thistles from a thorn bush!

having many people perform on a single day guarantees a really long recess!) One of Suzy's favorite things to watch during performances are the lips of the shyest kids mouthing the words as their classmate recites. She knows that in the coming months these reluctant public speakers will be making their "Big Fat Hen" debut.

The benefits of this challenge are many. Most significantly, it provides an opportunity for students to accomplish a difficult task that not only demonstrates their commitment to learning, but also benefits the group. Throughout the year, Suzy tries to provide many opportunities for individual achievement from which the whole community profits.

"Big Fat Hen" also focuses students' attention on the playful nature of language. All year, as students study ways to use words, Suzy introduces activities that show how fun and surprising language can be.

Memorizing "Big Fat Hen," like any memorization

Engaging Language Activities

- Find as many words as possible that contain the word "ant." Read the book *Ant: The Definitive Guide* by Jesse Tilly for examples. Challenge families to spend one week finding as many "ant" words as possible and bring the results to class.

- Study interesting words such as *megapod* (big feet), *soporific* (sleep-inducing), *triskadekaphobia* (fear of the number 13).

- Study word palindromes and keep a list of great examples. Read *Go Hang a Salami! I'm a Lasagna Hog!* by Jon Agee, and *Too Hot to Hoot: Funny Palindrome Riddles* by Marvin Terban.

- Play Spelling Baseball. Divide the class into two teams. Set up "bases" inside the room. Spellers stand at home plate and are "pitched" a word. If they spell it correctly, they go to first base. Some words qualify as doubles, triples, or home runs based on difficulty. Teammates can collaborate once per inning for help with spelling.

  Vocabulary Baseball is a more challenging version. Each student is pitched a definition of a word the class has been studying. If he gives the word that matches the meaning, he advances a base. Again, more challenging words qualify as doubles, triples, or homers.

- Do an author study of books by Ogden Nash.

- Plan a Limerick Week: Read lots of limericks, write your own, and invite other classes to a Limerick Open Mike.

activity, helps students learn tricks for committing words to memory, which can help them in academic tasks such as studying for tests, performing in poetry readings, and learning multiplication facts. And while earning extra recess minutes for the class is an altruistic goal, students who recite "Big Fat Hen" always walk away also feeling an enormous sense of personal pride.

It's not an easy challenge, yet throughout the year, to the final day of school, about 90 percent of the class memorizes and performs the poem for the group. And the 10 percent who don't memorize and perform the poem are not the shy kids or even the special education kids, who always seem to rise to the challenge—especially after hearing their peers perform it multiple times. They are the kids who are simply not motivated by the challenge. Most

Great Word Books

Who Ordered the Jumbo Shrimp? And Other Oxymorons by Jon Agee (HarperCollins)

Animalia by Graeme Base (Harry N. Abrams)

Four Famished Foxes and Fosdyke by Pamela Duncan Edwards (HarperTrophy)

Many Luscious Lollipops: A Book About Adjectives by Ruth Heller (and others in this series) (Grosset & Dunlap)

Watch William Walk by Ann Jonas (Greenwillow)

The Play of Words: Fun and Games for Language Lovers by Richard Lederer (Pocket Books)

CDB by William Steig (Simon and Schuster)

Funny You Should Ask: How to Make Up Jokes and Riddles with Word Play by Marvin Terban (Houghton Mifflin)

In a Pickle: And Other Funny Idioms by Marvin Terban (Houghton Mifflin)

of them have strong language skills and no problem standing up in front of the group; the task is just not their thing.

First Goodbye: A Fitting Farewell

Like all kids on their first day, Suzy's students go home on the first day with a backpack full of administrative papers to have signed and return. Getting this done is the first homework assignment of the year. The second one is connected to the All About Us board. Suzy reminds students to think about what they might bring in to start filling their squares. These two tasks are manageable and get students thinking about the importance of being ready for the next day. Fifth graders, like other upper-elementary students, need months of coaching before the homework routine becomes a daily habit. Spending time practicing these organizational skills is critical to students' academic and social success—and could speed up the process of forming good homework habits.

As the first month progresses, managing homework becomes a major focus. At the front of the room, Suzy hangs a 3- by 4-foot laminated poster of a homework organizer sheet. Her students have a stack of the same sheet, an 8½- by 11-inch version, in a homework binder. (See sample, left.)

Any time an assignment is given during the day, Suzy writes the task in the appropriate place on the poster. Students are then expected to copy this information onto their own sheets. At the end of the day, Suzy circulates around

| Name | Tristan M. | Date | 10-2 |

Homework Organizer

Monday	What To Do	When It's Due
Math	Choose 3 stocks from Nyse	Tuesday
Spelling/Vocabulary	Review words for test	Friday
Reading and Writing	Brainstorm research ideas	Wednesday
Social Studies	NONE	—
Science	find a butterfly cacoon	Friday

Tuesday	What To Do	When It's Due
Math	consult internet for stocks info	Friday
Spelling/Vocabulary	Choose 5 words for spelling	Wednesday
Reading and Writing	Finish literature circle reading	
Social Studies		
Science		

Wednesday	What To Do	When It's Due
Math		
Spelling/Vocabulary	Use 5 words in a sentance	Thursday
Reading and Writing	Revise Poem draft	
Social Studies		
Science		

Thursday	What To Do	When It's Due
Math		
Spelling/Vocabulary	Review my list for test	Friday
Reading and Writing		
Social Studies	Bring in biography on Civil War person	Monday
Science		

Friday	What To Do	When It's Due
Math		
Spelling/Vocabulary		
Reading and Writing	Read my independant book	Every Day
Social Studies	Think about my diorama plan	Monday
Science		

Scholastic Professional Books   The Back-to-School Book, Grades 3–6

Name _____   Date _____

Homework Organizer

Monday	What To Do	When It's Due
Math		
Spelling/Vocabulary		
Reading and Writing		
Social Studies		
Science		

Tuesday	What To Do	When It's Due
Math		
Spelling/Vocabulary		
Reading and Writing		
Social Studies		
Science		

Wednesday	What To Do	When It's Due
Math		
Spelling/Vocabulary		
Reading and Writing		
Social Studies		
Science		

Thursday	What To Do	When It's Due
Math		
Spelling/Vocabulary		
Reading and Writing		
Social Studies		
Science		

Friday	What To Do	When It's Due
Math		
Spelling/Vocabulary		
Reading and Writing		
Social Studies		
Science		

the room, checking each student's sheet and making sure he or she has written the task correctly and has the materials needed to complete it.

As a rule, Suzy gives homework three days a week. The assignments take thirty minutes to an hour to complete and often involve the whole family—such as reading aloud, practicing math facts, sharing a piece of writing, or collecting artifacts for a school project—with the understanding that evenings are busy and parents might not have a lot of time to spend on homework. The ideal assignment, in Suzy's mind, is one that helps parents get a feel for what their children are learning and thinking about at school. Family participation in this work is welcome, but not necessary. Discussion is the main goal.

Along with checking on homework at the end of the day, Suzy asks students to do a few jobs. Working together as a group to keep the room in order is an important community builder. By taking care of the space they call their own, starting from the very first day, students demonstrate a commitment to it. So Suzy asks everyone to pick up ten things from the floor that belong in the garbage—there are always more than enough punched-out holes, twisted paper clips, and tenacious staples lodged in the rug nap to keep the class busy. Students whose names are on the duty list are reminded to water plants, straighten books, erase the board, and stack chairs.

On day one, and throughout the year, Suzy also tries to touch base with each student before he or she leaves. Some children need lots of attention to get out the door in one piece. Others just need to hear a kind word about something they did during the day, or a good-luck wish for their piano recital or soccer game. Suzy stands in the doorway as bus dismissals are called to make sure she doesn't miss anyone. She feels satisfied sending the students off to their "other" world and ready for them to return the next morning.

Closing Thoughts

After the students have spilled out of the classroom toward their buses, car pools, and walks home, exhaustion and exhilaration battle for emotional supremacy. A good first day will have that effect, giving you the feeling that you've lived an entire school year in a single day. But the next day will be a fresh beginning—one that's full of repeated rituals, a few new rules, and some questions—but with a feeling of ownership and belonging that was just emerging on the first day.

For Suzy, the second day is the beginning of a journey toward open house, her class's first opportunity to debut as a community of learners and friends.

Chapter 3

Going Public

Energizing Open House

"Small cheer and great welcome makes a merry feast." • *William Shakespeare*

Light jazz plays softly from a boom box in the corner. The mood is festive, with clusters of students and adults in designated spots throughout the classroom. A mom wanders into an area festooned with signs indicating that it's a place for writing, and a student greets her. "Hi, welcome to writing workshop. I'm Bekka and here's what you're gonna do. You can write anything you want, but you have to be writing … or drawing. You can work with someone else, too, if you want," she explains, helping the mom blend into a group of adults already writing away. "And you don't have to worry too much about your spelling 'cause you can edit it later. We'll share in a few minutes." Kyle is holding a discussion on a read aloud of a chapter he just read to his group of parents, and Mark is asking his group of parents to share their thinking strategies as they solve a mathematical problem. "You can't just say, 'I did it in my head' either. You have to write about how you solved it," he reminds his group.

These are typical moments from the October open house in Jill Ostrow's fourth- to sixth-grade multi-age classroom. Students greet parents at the door and lead them to one of three areas in the room set up to demonstrate activities related to math, writing, and reading and calendar. When they enter the room, parents are given a checklist of areas to visit and activities to complete. Students in each area lead parents through mini-versions of workshops. For example, in the writing workshop area, parents complete brief drafts of writing and share them with each other. In the math area, another small group completes a set of mathematical problems designed by students. At the end of open house, all the parents gather together for a group sharing session to discuss what they experienced at each workshop. The students answer questions about what they did during the open house and what they experience daily in the classroom.

Jill's open house captures what is possible when we give upper-elementary students more responsibility for carrying out the event. You may wonder why we've chosen to devote a whole chapter to what is usually a one-time event. The reason is pretty simple. Open house gives you the opportunity to showcase the spirit of your classroom, demonstrate how students work together, and express the roles you want parents to have in the school community. It may be a one-time event, but memories of it (both good and bad) can linger throughout the year in students' homes.

Many families have mixed emotions about school based on their own classroom experiences. They may be uncertain about their relationship with you, the teacher. And that uncertainty can grow as students move up the grades and become more independent. Open house gives you a chance to stem parents' concerns and establish clear connections between your goals for the classroom and for the home.

From the moment you meet your students and begin working with them, it's hard to resist thinking about open house. As you plan, ask yourself:

- What do I want families to know about our class when they leave?

- What feeling do I want to convey about teaching and learning in our class?

- How will I know if the open house is a success?

Answering these questions will help you establish your goals for the event. For example, if you are a new teacher and concerned that parents will wonder about your experience and maturity, you might want to emphasize the curriculum at your open house. You can prepare handouts that outline your plans in subject areas, your systems for evaluation, or links between your curriculum and the state or district standards. Or you might arrive at a completely different goal: helping parents who have had little success in schools feel comfortable in your classroom so they will visit often. These parents might need a fun activity or two to break the ice.

Luckily, open house is a tradition that goes back decades in schools across the country. As a result, there are many variations in structure, timing, and content to choose from, and loads of resources to help in your planning. Let's explore some together.

Choosing the Right Time for Open House

There are three times early in the year to consider for open house: before school begins, during the first week, and in the middle of the fall, after routines have been established. We realize that many schools require that teachers follow dates and procedures. But if your school allows a choice, weigh the benefits of the different options.

Before the School Year Begins

The most non-threatening time of year for an open house is probably before the school year begins. You can use an open house as a drop-in period for families and students to help organize the room, choose desks or work spaces, or sign up for chores and responsibilities before the school year begins. (See Chapter 1.) Picnics, pot lucks, and barbecues are also good ways to ease into the school year. (See box below.)

The biggest advantage of this option is its informality. It gives parents a chance to talk with you in a relaxed setting, before the busy start of the school year. It also gives students and their families a role in setting up the classroom.

During the First Week

Open house during the first week of school allows parents to bring questions and concerns about your schedules and style to you as they emerge. Clearing up confusion at this point saves many teachers from dealing with the same questions and concerns over and over again, on an individual basis.

Open house in the first week of school can be hectic, however, given everything else you're trying to accomplish. But since you know students a bit at this point, you can give them some responsibility for preparations. And since your academic routines will be in place to some degree, students can also guide parents through the room and explain basic procedures.

In the Middle of the Fall

An open house later in the fall gives families a chance to see the classroom in full bloom. At that point, there will be lots of work on the walls. Most likely, students will be eager to show families what they know about the classroom and school. They can do more than give tours—they can perform skits, demonstrate how work is accomplished, and explain routines.

Open House in the Open Air

Some open houses don't take place in school at all. Consider hosting a picnic, pot luck, or barbecue on school grounds or a local park the Friday before the first week of school. It gives you a chance to see students interact with families and to build rapport with families in a natural setting.

I hope you can join us
for our before-school

Open House
Barbeque

at 6 PM
Thursday, August 20th
Samuels Field

(We'll meet at the pavilion near the softball field.)

I'll supply hotdogs, hamburgers, and veggie burgers. If you'd like to contribute, please bring your favorite salad or vegetable if your last name begins in A–S, and a dessert if your name begins in T–Z. The whole family is invited— bring siblings and grandparents if they are able to attend.

I'll see you soon!

Ms. Power

Sample invitation for an open-air open house

Open House Dos and Don'ts

- Provide refreshments. You can solicit parents for contributions the week before, if you like.

- Make sure student work is displayed prominently.

- Give a glimpse of life in your classroom with a video of the class at work or with student skits and presentations.

- Make it fun—student skits, scavenger hunts, and/or role plays will energize the event and provoke laughter.

- Don't get trapped into one-on-one conferences with parents. Quickly and firmly tell the parents that this is not the best place to discuss any individual student's needs. You might even have a sign-up form available with conference times for the following week.

- Don't give long-winded explanations of class rules and procedures. You can just as easily provide this information on a handout.

- Don't do all the work yourself. By the upper-elementary grades, students can and should take on much of the responsibility for presenting their work, designing bulletin boards, and guiding parents through the classroom.

- Don't solicit parents for classroom supplies and materials. We know it's popular to have a "giving tree" displayed (with requests for classroom contributions, written on leaves or apples that parents can pluck). We oppose this practice because, too often, it makes families that can't afford to help feel awkward.

Many teachers we know do a second open house, immediately before or after a school-wide event, just for the families of their students. They find that parents—especially those with more than one child in the school—appreciate the chance to spend extended time in the classroom, instead of rushing from room to room during the school-wide event.

Ensuring a Large Turnout

Concerned that no one will show up? Here are some strategies that are guaranteed to increase attendance:

✔ Send home a personal note with each student.

✔ Have students write and decorate personal invitations and mail them to family members from school.

✔ Make a quick phone call two or three nights before the open house to parents you suspect won't attend.

Responsibilities Students Can Take On for Open House

Before the event:

- Bring in refreshments.
- Design bulletin boards.
- Create invitations.

At the event:

- Give class tours.
- Present their work.
- Serve refreshments.
- Role play aspects of classroom life—for example, how they resolve conflicts or how they help each other in math.
- Perform skits.

Making Families Feel Welcome and Excited

Family members may be uncomfortable when they enter the classroom, so it's important to plan what happens right from that moment. You may want to be at the door greeting them. In case you miss a few because you're busy with other guests, have a handout ready for a student greeter to distribute at the door. The handout should outline the schedule for the night or direct guests in a friendly way to different areas of the room or materials they might want to browse. Below are a few other ideas for making families feel comfortable.

Scavenger Hunt

A scavenger hunt is a popular activity for getting guests moving through the room and meeting one another. This can be done the traditional way, by distributing a list of about twenty objects and/or facts (e.g., the color of the math folders), with instructions for guests to try to find each one.

However, a "Family Scavenger Hunt" is even more fun. In the week or two before open house, have students write autobiographies or interview their parents for some family history. Then, have each student choose a fact about himself or herself to add to the list, such as "This student's grandmother immigrated from Croatia in 1953," or "This is the only student in the class with three brothers." At the open house, distribute the list to guests and have them talk to each other to determine which facts apply to which students. Award small prizes to the first adult and first child to guess all the clues correctly.

A variation on "Family Scavenger Hunt" is "Name Game Scavenger Hunt." In the days before the open house, students interview their parents about why they were given their names and translate the information into scavenger-hunt clues: "Named after grandmother" or "Named after Dad's favorite singer," for example. This is a terrific way to help parents remember the names of many children in the classroom.

Videos, Slide Shows, and Photo Displays

You can give families a feel for the classroom community without resorting to long, boring recitations of daily activities. Prepare a brief slide show or video—no more than five to ten minutes—of classroom routines. Here's how:

1. Before open house, videotape or photograph

students at work in the morning and afternoon. Make sure you keep a class list handy to check who's made it on camera. You may want to tape or photograph over two days to ensure you capture all students.

2. During open house, narrate the video or slide show as it plays, touching on important daily activities and responsibilities of students.

3. Play soft music that captures the moods you try to create in the classroom.

4. If you don't have access to audiovisual equipment, create a gallery. Take photographs of students at work, have students write captions that emphasize curricular expectations, and post the photos on a bulletin board.

A quick visual presentation is a wonderful way to give families the flavor of life in your classroom.

Student Performances

One way to promote attendance at the first open house is to schedule a performance. Seeing their child on stage is a powerful motivator for parents, and most upper-elementary students thrill to the call of the stage.

In Suzy Kaback's classroom, dramatic poetry and short, humorous skits are featured events at open house. Her fifth graders often use Paul Fleischman's books of poems for two voices, *Joyful Noise* and *I Am Phoenix*. Pairs of students choose a poem and practice tandem reading in the weeks preceding open house. Suzy's students might also perform two- to three-minute skits to entertain visitors.

One week before open house, invitations are sent home announcing the performance as a marquee event for the evening. On the night of the open house, the performance begins a half hour after the arrival time, which gives families a chance to take a brief tour and get settled in chairs that the class arranged audience-style beforehand. The space turns hot quickly, and there isn't much elbow room, but that doesn't stop families from enjoying their children on stage.

Productions like these highlight the sense of community that infuses the classroom. And the families typically support the efforts of Suzy and her students.

Resources for Open House Performances

Easy Skits and Plays:

On Stage: Theater Games and Activities for Kids by Lisa Bany-Winters (Chicago Review Press)

Mystery Plays: 8 Plays for the Classroom by Tom Conklin (Scholastic)

Drama in the Classroom: Creative Activities for Teachers, Parents & Friends by Polly Erion (Lost Coast Press)

The Skit Book: 101 Skits from Kids by Margaret Read MacDonald (Shoe String Press)

Read-Aloud Plays: Tall Tales by Carol Pugliano-Martin (Scholastic)

101 Drama Games for Children: Fun and Learning With Acting and Make-Believe by Paul Rooyackers, et al (Hunter House Smartfun Book)

Performance Poetry:

A Joyful Noise: Poems for Two Voices by Paul Fleischman (Harper & Row)

I Am Phoenix: Poems for Two Voices by Paul Fleischman (Harper & Row)

http://www.poetism.com/links/poetry_for_kids.html

Most years they get 100 percent attendance. Many parents arrive with camcorders, which they don't bring to typical show-and-tell gatherings. Suzy attributes high attendance to the academic *and* social focus of the evening.

Web Resources for Planning Open House

For more practical tips to help you design a terrific open house, we recommend the following Web sites:

http://www.atozteacherstuff.com/tips/Back_to_School/Open_House-Orientation
Tips by and for teachers at all grade levels.

http://www.inspiringteachers.com/tips/openhouse.html
Resources that are especially helpful to new teachers who are hosting their first open house.

http://www.education-world.com/a_admin/admin240.shtml
Open house from an administrator's perspective, with checklists that are helpful to teachers.

http://www.publicengagement.com/tools/standards/engaging/openhouse
Suggestions for an open house designed to help parents understand how to look at student work and curricular standards.

http://www.teachervision.com/lesson-plans/lesson-6522.html
Useful tools such as handouts, letters to send home, and even a sign to hang on the door.

Following Up After the Event

According to fourth-grade teacher Janet Nordfors, finishing the first day of school is like finishing Thanksgiving dinner—she feels overstuffed, over-stimulated, and has a lot of clean-up and thinking to do before plunging into the next day. We feel the same way after open house. There is so much to take in, so much to mull over about family relationships when we see our students with parents.

We've found it's always worth the time to correspond with parents after open house, highlighting what we enjoyed about meeting them. You can send a full letter to everyone, mentioning favorite moments (and making sure that each student is somehow included). Or you can send a shorter note, with room at the bottom for a brief, personal thank you. Either way, the connections you make can lead to more thoughtful and individualized relationships with families all year long.

Closing Thoughts

Open house may be a one-time event, but it always reminds us that we are only a part of a network of people who are working with our students. Connections to families help us do our jobs better because they give us a better sense of students' histories and the support that is available to them at home. It's rare to find a child who isn't dearly loved by at least one person at home. Open houses remind us of that truth.

Chapter 4

Community

Creating Safe, Respectful, and Caring Environments

"It is not enough to be busy, so are the ants. The question is:

What are we busy about?" ● *Henry David Thoreau*

Throughout this book we've stressed the importance of building a community. In the busy-ness of classroom life, it is not always easy to take the time to nurture relationships among students, to stop a lesson when a student is disrespectful to a peer and iron out differences, or to bring problems related to routines or assignments to the whole class for discussion.

But paying attention to these aspects of classroom life, especially in the first days and weeks of school, determines whether a class becomes a real community instead of lots of busy individuals focused on one task after another. Lest any of us forget the words of education expert Linda Darling-Hammond: "… many special features of teaching make relationships important. Children and teachers do not choose one another; furthermore, teachers cannot succeed unless students are willing to put forth effort to learn and unless the entire group is working productively."

The teachers we collaborate with in Brewer, Maine, all work hard to create safe, respectful, and caring communities. In this chapter, we want to share some practical tips we've learned from them and others. In the end, real classroom community has the potential to foster real learning. It is more than "feel good" window dressing. In fact, research links the creation of classroom community to positive academic, social, and personal attitudes; class engagement; and academic achievement (Osterman, 2000).

Creating a Community of Caring

The Brewer school district uses the "Community of Caring" program in all classrooms to promote trust and support. Developed by the Joseph P. Kennedy Foundation, the program works to encourage and help teachers implement five values in schools throughout the country:

1. Caring
2. Respect
3. Responsibility
4. Trust
5. Family

The program offers extensive free resources on the Internet, such as online staff development and a newsletter. To learn more, check out:

http://www.communityofcaring.org

By the time they reach the upper-elementary grades, students in Brewer are quite familiar with the goals and aims of the program because they have had extensive experience with activities aimed at promoting its values.

While the Community of Caring program is terrific, it is only one of many that you might adopt in your

Other Programs for Character- and Community-Building

- *The Character Education Partnership* (CEP) is a nonpartisan coalition of organizations and individuals dedicated to developing moral character and civic virtues in youth. CEP's Web site (http://www.character.org) has an online discussion of character education, character education news, and character education questions and answers, as well as links to other character education sites.

- *The Center for the 4th and 5th Rs* encourages respect and responsibility. The center's Web site (http://www.cortland.edu/www/c4n5rs) has helpful information about character education, including newsletters and a comprehensive school/community survey.

- *The Institute for Global Ethics* promotes ethical behavior in individuals, institutions, and nations. The institute has developed curricula for upper-elementary and middle-level students. Its Web site (http://www.globalethics.org) contains sample lessons that you can download at no cost. It also has an ethics news line which reports worldwide news with an ethical component—a wonderful resource for current events activities.

own classroom to foster respect and open dialogue. (See box on page 82.) Community building is about more than activities, after all. It's about creating a climate where every voice is heard, and civility is an expectation for all.

Talking to Students and Teachers About the Importance of Community

We surveyed all fifth graders in one Brewer school to get their perspective, in their own words, about what they valued and felt mattered most for success in school. Sure enough, "belonging" or "sense of community" was high on the list for almost everyone.

Students were eloquent in their assertions that a focus on respect, caring, responsibility, and trust in their classrooms helps them to learn for three important reasons:

1. **A sense of community decreased distractions.** As one child said, "No one is swearing, and talking, and disrespecting the teacher." Another said, "People don't distract other people during class. They respect other people's space, care about learning."

2. **A sense of community helped students feel safe**, as this exchange suggests: "In our class you don't laugh at a person if they make a mistake." "Yeah, it's true." "Yeah, it is trust and family." "It's respect, too, because they tried their best." "And it is your responsibility to do that [not laugh]."

3. **A sense of community made students feel respected, trusted, capable, and responsible.** "The teachers give respect and they say you can actually do it when you say you can't. They know you really can," stressed one student. "We have learned to work together," said another. "You trust another person with helping you with things, to help you learn. You trust them not to cheat."

In separate interviews, teachers stated that their classroom communities—which were based on respect, trust, caring, and responsibility—enhanced student learning for similar reasons. They, too, claimed community minimizes distractions: "If you have that respectful tone in your classroom, then the things that could get in the way of learning aren't there," one teacher told us. "You can focus more on learning." Teachers also noted community's importance in helping students become more independent and responsible: "… with kids getting their homework done and being responsible for it, I think community is a big part," one said. Another insisted, "Kids that don't feel respected will close up. They are not going to be with you, and I don't see how they'll learn. So if you are in an environment where it feels safe, where it feels like family, where you feel your ideas are respected, you are starting at the right point."

Translating Respectful Beliefs Into Actions

In a recent issue of *Education Week*, Judith Yero asserts many of the important qualities of effective teachers are elusive because they are in the mind and cannot be observed. However, those qualities determine how a teacher acts, what she says, and, therefore, how she develops her classroom environment. Yero concludes that effective teachers share the following characteristics:

- A belief that all children can learn, but not in the same way.

- A belief that teachers are learners and that children are teachers.

- A high level of respect for all students.

- High expectations for all students, but not the same for all.

- A humanistic rather than custodial approach to classroom control.

Setting the Tone for Community in the Classroom

Teachers who build safe, respectful, and trusting communities convey, in all they say and do, a tone that derives from their affection for children and their belief that those children are capable and important. That tone comes through in many ways, such as in the way they express their expectation and trust that students will behave, rather than resorting to arbitrary rules. It comes through in their explanations to students of why certain rules are necessary for the class to be successful, and in dealing with behavior issues when they do arise. And it's shown by their willingness to listen to students, provide some choices, and discuss class issues and solve class problems with students. Here are some general guidelines for setting the right tone in your classroom.

Avoid Comparing Students

The teachers we've worked with in Brewer do their best to avoid an age-old tendency: comparing students. Step into many of their kindergarten and first-grade classrooms and you are likely to hear a teacher say something such as, "I like the way Janette is sitting in her place for morning meeting." Typically the rest of the students will then fall into place to please the teacher. But using a comment like that in the upper grades can embarrass the student who is picked out. A teacher might say instead, "Class, please check that you are sitting the way we agreed would work for morning meeting." The tone of the message is then one that reflects a group decision about what worked best, a compact between teachers and students.

Ask for Ideas From Students

Another way teachers set a tone for community building is to ask for ideas from students regularly. In discussions, they pose questions such as, "What do you think?" "How else could we solve that problem?" "Do you agree? Why or why not?" Student opinions and thoughts are encouraged in a calm, interested tone, which fosters rich discussion.

Model Respectful Language

Teachers from Brewer also notice students. They tell students they like them. They greet students as they enter the classroom and check on how they are doing. They make comments to students, such as, "I am so glad you are here today. We missed you yesterday." "You are such a great class." "How are you today?" Students are important to them—and their words and actions prove it. They model what they believe. And by so doing, they set a respectful tone.

Tips for Creating Classroom Rules With Students

Here's some advice from veteran teachers on forming rules with students:

1. Brainstorm possible rules with the class. As you form the list, keep asking "Why?" This reinforces the fact that rules have a reason: to make students feel safe, comfortable, and valued. Asking why also prevents students from coming up with arbitrary rules and harsh punishments.

2. Post students' responses in a place where they can be viewed by all—on chart paper or the board.

3. Come up with no more than three rules in the first week. Add to the list slowly, as the need for new rules emerges.

4. If the class misses an essential rule, don't hesitate to add it. Just be sure to explain why you have found this rule helpful in the past.

5. Revise the rules throughout the first weeks of school. This shows the whole class that the community is a work in progress—and so is the set of rules that govern the community.

Whole-Class Meetings

Upper-elementary students need a predictable routine that helps them know what to expect and, therefore, to feel safe. Regularly scheduled whole-class meetings should be a part of that routine; they are an essential part of building community. Most teachers with whom we work plan two kinds of whole-class meetings: morning meetings and problem-solving meetings. We will discuss both in this section.

At the start of the year, establish procedures for all whole-class meetings, such as the ones that follow. When you discuss procedures with students and give them a voice in creating them, students are more likely to feel invested in them. This kind of open communication around expectations also allows you to remind students, when necessary, that the whole class chose the procedures for good reason.

● COMMUNICATING

Here are some questions to ask yourself—and your students—to get healthy communication going:

- *What is the appropriate way to greet people?* Fifth-grade teacher Dennis Levesque has students greet one another by making eye contact, shaking hands, and saying good morning using their classmates' names. He models the behavior on day one by greeting each student by name and shaking his or her hand.

- *What does a good listener do?* We've found that most children know what a good listener looks and sounds like and will gladly adopt the receptive attitude needed to become one. "Sitting quietly" usually suffices.

- *What does a good sharer do?* All students have been the "victims" of classmates going on too long. Teachers need to suggest that, in order to get through all that needs to be accomplished every day, comments and questions must be brief. You might establish a procedure that sets limits somehow, such as asking for only three comments by the sharer and three questions from the listeners.

● TURN TAKING

Who gets to speak in a class meeting is a big issue for most upper-elementary students because they believe strongly in fairness. Here are a few ideas for ways to take turns:

- Choose sharers in order, by simply going around the circle to the right one day and to the left the next. Students can pass if they do not want to say anything.

- Pick sharers alphabetically by their first initial or any other objective way.

- Be gender neutral. Some teachers require that sharers alternate between girls and boys when calling on listeners for comments or questions. If the sharer calls on a girl first, he or she must choose a boy next.

● MOVING ON

What is the procedure for making the transition from the meeting to the next activity of the day? There is no single best procedure, but having one for each type of whole-class meeting brings quick closure to the meeting and a quick transition to the next activity.

- For morning meeting, the last activity might be checking the schedule for the day. This serves as a signal for students to return to their seats and start the first activity on the schedule.

- For the problem-solving meeting, the last activity might be a statement from you such as, "We have discussed the issue and decided on a solution. Is everyone here ready to follow what we decided?" If students agree, they can move on to the next activity.

Morning Meeting

Whole-class morning meeting sets the tone for the day. We find that seating students in a circle works best. It facilitates good communication because students can see one another and no one gets a preferential position.

GATHERING

Morning meeting should last no more than 10 to 15 minutes, especially if students are taught procedures for gathering quickly. For example, on the first day of school, Janet Nordfors has her fourth graders form a circle once. She then asks them to try it again, this time timing them with a stopwatch. Then, she has them try it one more time to see if they can beat their time. Of course, throughout the activity she encourages students to be cautious. Stephen Bearor, a fifth- and sixth-grade teacher, does the same activity with his students. Trying to cut off seconds is fun and a community builder, since students are working together to decrease time.

GREETING

It's important for each child to greet someone and be greeted back. This practice teaches social skills and prompts students to recognize one another. There are many types of greetings, from shaking hands to giving an introduction in a language other than English to giving high fives all around.

When you run out of new ideas for greetings, teacher Carol Davis suggests asking your students to come up with variations on the ones you use. One of her students came up with the "say your name" twist, which is great for the beginning of the year. In this greeting, the whole class chants, "Say your name and when you do, we will say it back to you." Then, the first child says his name and the whole class repeats the name in unison. The whole class chants the refrain again, and the next student says her name. This greeting helps students learn each other's names fast! As a variation, students can use a deep, soft, or high voice to say their name, and the class echoes that voice. Also, students can add a gesture or movement as they say their name, which the class mimics, or they might add clapping.

Another suggestion, from Susan Roser, is the "closed-eye greeting." All students close their eyes and the teacher says "Good morning, Mariette." Mariette opens her eyes and says good morning to another student who then opens his eyes. The greeting continues until all eyes are open. Susan suggests this greeting be used after students know and trust each other.

These and other morning meeting greetings can be found in the fall 2000 *Responsive Classroom* newsletter at www.responsiveclassroom.org.

After gathering and greeting, go over the schedule for the day with the class, announcing and writing any changes on the board. You can devote the rest of the morning meeting to various topics according to the time of year, the needs of students, and your goals. You can use it as a sharing time or news time, focusing on one or two students, or you can play a game with an academic slant. You can also encourage skill building through role playing different situations, or celebrate the class's progress and successes.

5th Grade Morning Meeting

A typical morning meeting in Dennis Levesque's class begins with students shaking hands around the circle and wishing one another good morning. Next, they play a game such as ABC. Students stand in a circle and, one by one, say a letter of the alphabet in order. If the letter a student says is the same as the first letter of her name, she must say her name and sit down. This continues until everyone sits down. ABC is especially appropriate at the beginning of the year because it helps students learn each other's names.

After the game, Dennis has the students look at a note on the white board, such as:

> High Kids
> Welcum to fifth grade!
> Wear going to have a great year.
> I hope you are ready to learn a lot!
> Sincerely,
> r. Levesque

Things to Watch for During Whole-Class Meetings

So how will you know if your students are growing emotionally, socially, and academically during class meetings? This kind of growth isn't always easy to measure. We like the tips in *Class Meetings: Building Leadership, Problem Solving and Decision Making Skills in the Respectful Classroom* (Pembroke/Stenhouse, 2001). Author Donna Styles recommends you watch to make sure that students are:

- Gaining self-confidence
- Complimenting one another
- Generating creative solutions
- "Piggybacking" on ideas from others
- Disagreeing with one another in a respectful manner
- Staying on task for longer periods of time

Talk with students about these goals and develop rubrics and other tools for measuring positive changes in behavior.

He then asks students to offer suggestions for correcting the note and to decide when there's no more work to be done.

Dennis ends the morning meeting each day with a sharing. On day one, he asks students: "What is the very first memory you have?" After the sharing, students return to their desks to begin the scheduled activities written on the board.

The morning meeting provides an opportunity for students to practice the rules and procedures of the day. Because it's predictable, it makes students feel comfortable and allows you to notice every child, every morning. Respect, routines, and recognition are the central themes.

And when those themes remain present, morning meeting helps to maintain community throughout the year.

Icebreakers

For tried and true icebreakers, we encourage you to visit "The Teacher's Corner" on the Internet at:

http://www.theteacherscorner.net/seasonal/backtoschool/index.htm#IntermediateGrades4-6

This site includes all-time favorites, such as "Passing Toilet Paper," and various name games, but it also has some unusual activities based on themes and famous people's birthdays, which can be lots of fun for students. All ideas were developed and submitted by teachers.

Problem-Solving Meetings

In a classroom community, everyone has the right and the responsibility to make the community safe and respectful. Whole-class problem-solving meetings provide opportunities to deal with difficult issues as they emerge—issues such as rough-housing at recess, computer hogging, or making unkind remarks. You can schedule meetings on a regular basis or as issues come up. The topic for discussion may be suggested by you; however, if problem-solving meetings become a regular event, you may want to hand the responsibility over to students.

3rd Grade Problem-Solving Meeting

Early in September, as they were preparing to enter the classroom, some of Ellen Fisher's third graders were saving spaces for themselves in line by using their backpacks. This upset other students, who felt it wasn't fair. So Ellen convened a class problem-solving meeting.

First, Ellen asked students to define the issue by explaining why saving a place with a backpack is good and why it is not. Students who thought it was good made comments such as, "We have to put our backpacks and lunchboxes somewhere, and putting them by the door in line is a good place. We have to line up there to come in." And students who disagreed replied, "But it isn't fair to hold a place in line. When the bell rings, we line up and whoever gets in line first should go in first."

Everyone who wanted to add a statement was encouraged to do so. Ellen summarized each side's arguments and asked for a vote of hands. Students voted to continue using backpacks to save places in line. However, a few days later complaints started emerging that some students were stepping on others' things because they were slow getting in line. So Ellen held a second problem-solving meeting. Again, she opened by having students define the issue, with the new dilemma added. From there, she went on to ask, "How do you think we can solve this problem so no one's belongings get damaged?"

One child suggested, "We could be more careful not to step on the backpacks."

Another said, "We could stop using the backpacks to save a place in line."

Ellen asked, "Where could we put the backpacks so that they're safe?" After more discussion it was decided, by a vote, to put all belongings in one location by the building rather than to hold spots in line with them. Ellen concluded the meeting by asking all students to remember and follow their new plan.

Ellen allowed the students to come up with solutions, rethink them, and try others. In the process, her students learned that they could solve problems in a fair way and, in doing so, they gained responsibility.

When the Rules Don't Work

Having trouble with one or two students who can't or won't follow the rules? Try "You Can Handle Them All" at http://www.discipline help.com. The site details over 100 different types of behavior problems, analyzing root problems and outlining a range of ways to work with students to integrate them into the classroom community. It also offers a free "Tip of the Week" e-newsletter, which is sent directly to subscribers.

Teaching Conflict Resolution and Problem-Solving Strategies

In *Waging Peace in Our Schools* (Beacon Press, 1996), Linda Lantieri and Janet Patti recognize that solving problems can be overwhelming. So they share a simple but effective four-step process they developed for students and teachers:

1. Explain the problem, without blaming, from several different points of view.
2. Brainstorm as many solutions as possible.
3. Decide what solutions are "good."
4. Choose one solution and try it.

Ways We Want Our Class to Be is another wonderful resource for teaching collective decision-making skills (Developmental Studies Center, 1996).

To help students perform their best in problem-solving meetings, practice with hypothetical, but realistic problems. And to make a real problem-solving meeting go smoothly, you may want to do a little work beforehand, such as speaking with a few kids to get them thinking about solutions or talking with a child who has been called names to help him or her rehearse how to explain how that feels. Solving problems as a class empowers students and provides practice in resolving conflicts on their own.

A few children may struggle with respectful and responsible community-building behaviors. Don't give up on them. You and the rest of the class must continue to model behaviors, which includes showing respect for the misbehaving child. The "You Can Handle Them All" Web site, which is described left, is a terrific site for tips on identifying and dealing with specific behavioral needs.

Resources for Conflict Resolution

Educators for Social Responsibility focus on peace making and conflict resolution. Their Web site (http://www.esrnational.org) contains free lesson plans and links to other peace-making and conflict-resolution Web sites.

Stark County Interdisciplinary Units This Web site (http://www.stark.k12.oh.us/Docs/units) offers interdisciplinary unit plans created by the teachers of Stark County, Ohio. Many of the units, such as "Youth Violence and Conflict Resolution the Peaceful Way," are directly related to dealing with discord in the classroom.

The Conflict Resolution Information Web Site (http://www.crinfo.org/k12.cfm) lists and describes many K-12 conflict resolution programs.

Closing Thoughts

When we dedicate ourselves to using a respectful tone, modeling responsibility, recognizing and caring for students, and involving them in morning- and problem-solving meetings, we create community. The classroom becomes a safe place for students and teachers—a place where it's easier for everyone to take risks. And risk taking in a safe environment is what learning is all about.

Chapter 5

Classroom Communication

Speaking the Language of Learning and Belonging

"I think a lot of our problems are because people don't listen to our children. It is not always easy. They're not always so brilliant that you want to spend hours with them. But it is very important to listen to them."

● *Barbara Bush*

Someone once said it's easy to make a classroom look good, but much harder to make it sound good. That person was probably talking about talking and listening.

We've spent most of this book helping you visualize what the first weeks of school might look and feel like. In this chapter, we'll explore what they might sound like as you help students learn to be independent. We will also take a look at language beyond the classroom and into the homes of students. How we communicate with children and families makes all the difference in establishing a community where the learning is thoughtful and deep.

Words in the air are the invisible glue that tie a classroom community together. Modeling for students in September how talking and listening work in your classroom may be your most challenging and important back-to-school task. And building an open-ended rapport with families can be an even greater challenge. But come December, it's not the layout of the room that will matter when you assess whether students can work well independently. It's the "talk curriculum"—the norms in place for the way you, students, and families discuss tasks—that will determine whether students can take more responsibility for their learning as the school year progresses.

Why Classroom Talk Matters

The amount and quality of talk in classrooms is tied directly to student learning and achievement (Allington and Cunningham, 1996). But many teachers are locked in the Initiation-Response-Evaluation (IRE) mode when speaking with students. For example, the teacher asks a simple question, such as, "Is it sunny outside today?" which requires a quick response from students. The teacher responds with an equally quick evaluative comment such as "You're right!" or "Good job!" before moving on to the next question or comment.

Certainly there are times when it makes sense to check in with students to get a sense if they are comprehending an idea or absorbing new information. But overuse of the IRE mode may lead students to expect that all responses to classroom questions are short and easily given—and evaluated solely by their teacher. IRE is not a formula for promoting either independence in students or a sense that many important questions in learning have no simple answers.

By the upper-elementary grades, students who are accustomed to this style of talk may find it hard to break out of it. Helping students learn to talk to each other in a different way should begin in the first days of school. Jill Ostrow accomplishes this with her fourth to sixth graders by having them interview each other. She distributes an interview sheet and has students partner up. (See next page.) Jill finds that this is a great way to kick off open-ended talk in her classroom. Students use the answers to these questions to begin drafting introductions of each other to the class.

This is the first of many tasks Jill assigns that show students that the language norms in her classroom will be different. Students are expected to ask rich questions, with no clear answers. They are also challenged to mull over responses and, when necessary, dig deeper for more information and clarity. Learning these language norms begins at a social level—kids are naturally interested in each others' lives—but Jill quickly extends them into the academic curriculum.

Partner Interview Sheet

Name: Kelsey

The name of who you are interviewing: Alexandria

Write down at least three questions you want to ask your partner. (Try to avoid questions that will only give you a yes/no answer.) Ask the questions and record your partner's answers.

What do you do for fun
I like to swim swing watch t.V.
Snorkel and I like to play softball I
Love to listen to Harry Potter tapes #4 The
goblet of fire is my Favorite
would you like to be my friend? Why
Yes because you're nice and generous
What did you do on you birth day last year
I went to a skating rink

What did you find surprising? What do you want to know more about?

nothing suprising Maybe if she had
any pets

Think of one more questions that you want to know more about.

do you have any pets

Ask that question but this time also record body language, voice, etc.

She got excited when I asked the pet
question She said I have 17 fish and a turtle
named Cullem

Draft a lead—two to three sentences—about this person.

Alex likes to be in the water She is
a nice person and she had a fun
birthday party last year and she has a
turtle

Partner Interview Sheet

Name: _____   Date: _____

The name of who you are interviewing:

Write down at least three questions you want to ask your partner. (Try to avoid questions that will only give you a yes/no answer.) Ask the questions and record your partner's answers.

What did you find surprising? What do you want to know more about?

Think of one more question that you want to know more about.

Ask that question but this time also record body language, voice, etc.

Draft a lead—two to three sentences—about this person.

Building a Better Talk Curriculum

The best way to judge if you've fallen into the IRE trap is to monitor your exchanges with students over a half hour or more in your classroom. How many questions do you ask that are open-ended? How many times does a student make a response that doesn't receive an evaluative comment from you? If the answer to either of these questions is rarely, you might want to spend a little time sprucing up your talk curriculum. Changing the language norms now in your classroom will reap big dividends throughout the year, as your students become more comfortable with complex questions and self-evaluation of their responses.

Learning new ways of talking with students in your classroom begins by applying some simple principles. You might want to work on them one at a time, each for a few weeks, to master the language of one before you move on to the next.

Avoid asking "yes/no" questions

When you find yourself starting to ask a question that requires a yes or no response, find a way to rephrase it so that it is open-ended. In their book *Thinking for Themselves: Developing Strategies for Reflective Learning* (Eleanor Curtain Publishers, 1993), Jeni Wilson and Lesley Wing Jan suggest routinely using these open-ended questions to help students think more deeply about their learning:

- What reasons do you have for that?
- How is that different from your classmate's idea?
- What have you based that on?
- How could you work it out if that were true?
- What do we know about this?
- What would be an example of this?
- When wouldn't that happen?
- How does this help us?
- How else could we think about that?
- What have we found out so far?

- What do you think about this?
- What do others think?
- I don't know. What do you think?

Devote time every day to telling stories

One of the best ways to build language skills is to share personal histories. It's also a natural way to build community and link home and school. One favorite conversation starter among teachers we know is to have students talk and write about the history of their names—how and why their parents picked their names. Franki Sibberson, a fourth-grade teacher in Dublin, Ohio, has children interview their parents about their favorite books, and then they share the information with the class.

Increase your wait time

As humorist Fran Lebowitz writes, "The opposite of talking is not listening. The opposite of talking is waiting." Adding just a few seconds onto your pause at the end of a question, particularly an open-ended question, gives students the time they need to think through complex answers. Remember, they might have spent years in school communicating in the IRE mode. Don't be surprised if they are confused at first by all your questions that have no easy answers. So wait. And wait. And wait for an answer. The longer you wait, the more you show a student you care about her response.

Develop one-on-one strategies for helping your challenging talkers

We develop individualized plans to help children who struggle with reading or who can barely put pencil to paper during writing workshop. Students who struggle with social interaction also need extra attention. For example, in group discussions, Adele Ames, a teacher in Brewer, Maine, uses a simple hand signal (closed fist, thumb up) with one talkative student to let him know he needs to wrap up his comments. The signal is unobtrusive, but effective in limiting his soliloquies.

Connecting School and Home

Establishing new ways of talking can change the way you see students and work with them. But a daunting question remains: How can we help families talk more with their children about learning—especially in ways that expand and extend what's going on the classroom?

Personalized Weekly Newsletters

One answer may be to model personal, positive, and continuous communication about learning with families. This is often easiest to accomplish in writing—writing that needn't take a large amount of time.

Fifth-grade teacher Suzy Kaback ends each week with "FYI," a newsletter. The body contains the traditional "what we're doing, where we're going" kind of message, but at the bottom she includes a two-inch space called the Weekly Update. In this space Suzy writes a positive, personal note about each student. If a student is way behind in her homework or is having trouble keeping his hands to himself, she doesn't use the newsletter to make it known. She makes a phone call instead.

The Weekly Update is a place to share accomplishments, both big and small. If a student proves to be a cooperative, efficient group member, Suzy makes a note of it. If the class enjoyed a student's opening moment that week, she makes sure the family knows of the success. When someone is making great progress in learning her multiplication facts, Suzy adds the compliment to the Weekly Update.

Writing a couple of sentences about each student takes about 45 minutes a week, and the rewards are significant. Students look forward to reading the little dose of weekly praise. They often share what Suzy wrote about them with each other. Because the news is always good, their weeks always end on a positive note.

Parents await the newsletter with equal interest. Suzy asks them to sign it each week and return it on Monday,

FYI Mrs. Kaback's Fifth Grade Class Newsletter

Welcome Back! We made a smooth transition into our school routine and everyone enjoyed hearing about the adventures of classmates during spring break. An interesting note to many parents … a lot of kids said the first Friday of vacation was their favorite day because younger siblings were in school at Holden or Eddington and they got to spend quality time alone with their parents. Interesting! It's always those little moments that make a difference!

creative garden design projects

The creative garden design projects look fantastic. It's easy to see that plenty of work was done creating interesting, fertile gardens. The variety of styles is impressive. We have bean seeds sprouting, terraria, rock gardens complete with pools of water, experiments with light, water and temperature, an elaborate self-watering planter that feeds four plants at one time, a garden built inside a house … the list goes on and on!

Thanks to families who sent in pictures of the garden's progress. These will be invaluable for charting the growth of each project.

Our Butterfly Garden is making slow, but noticeable progress. We have constructed a bin to contain a compost pile, so when you have grass cuttings to contribute we'll gladly accept them. Manure is also a precious commodity. We'll take any extra you have!

New Book: The Search for Delicious

We've begun a new book called *The Search for Delicious* by Natalie Babbitt. (She's the author of *Tuck Everlasting*, a classic many of you may know.) It's a wonderful story set in medieval times about a boy who has been charged with the duty of preventing civil war by finding kingdom-wide agreement on the definition of the word delicious. The study of word origins is only one of the important features of this book. I have plenty of extra copies, so please read along and join us for literature circles if you can!

Coming Soon … Our Memoirs

Our memoirs are in the final stages of writing. It's our homeroom's turn to use the computer lab daily, so we're spending plenty of time word processing to get our work looking professional. We will soon publish our favorite pieces in a collection of classroom prose which we plan to send home for family enjoyment.

> *Book orders were sent home on Monday, April 22. The deadline for ordering is* **Friday, May 3.**

WEEKLY UPDATE

John has had a great week. His memoir is completed and word processed, so he's been helping classmates finish by adding graphics & other stylish features. This week he was the discussion header in his literature circle—he manages discussions very well! Great job!

and the response rate is always high. In fact, parents often write back to her. She keeps these exchanges in a big notebook of parent communication.

If Suzy misses a week, she's usually faced with a barrage of requests on Monday, asking if the newsletter was overlooked, lost, or forgotten. This reaction signals the value of the weekly updates, especially for parents who often feel underinformed about their children's school lives.

The most beneficial part of the weekly update for Suzy, though, is sitting down each week and thinking carefully about each student. This practice keeps Suzy feeling like she has her finger on the pulse of the class. If she has to dig deep to think of something to write about a particular child, she sees it as a red flag that maybe that child is slipping between the cracks a little. Suzy makes a mental note to spend extra time with that student in the coming week. Writing a weekly update is one way to improve those statistics by showing students that we are paying attention and concerned, even when we can't be everywhere at once.

Math Backpacks

Homework is often a chore not only for upper-elementary students, but for their parents, as well. Usually parents wind up supervising the task, rather than becoming involved in it with their children or using it as an opportunity to chat about learning in an open way. Breaking away from traditional assignments might help. Tasks that are open-ended, fun, and collaborative encourage family members to talk more with their children about school. Suzy, for example, designed the math backpack, a large bag filled with a variety of math games, books, and supplies.

Each student takes the math backpack home once during each quarter of the school year. He or she signs up on a calendar, which helps Suzy keep track of who has taken the backpack home and who will down the

Items in a Math Backpack

- Games such as mancala, Uno, math bingo, Yahtzee, and Set
- Tangrams
- Blank bingo boards and markers
- Geoboards
- Dice
- Calculators
- Rulers
- Protractors
- Compasses
- Index cards with math challenges written on them, for example: "Measure the circumference of five round things in your house," "Try to arrive at the value of pi," "Conduct a survey—think of an interesting question and poll at least ten people. Present the results in writing and on a graph."
- Flashcards
- Graph paper
- Colored pencils
- Books such as *Math Curse, The Librarian Who Measured the Earth,* and *G Is for Googol*
- A composition notebook

line. Whoever has the backpack for the night is exempt from other math homework, making the activity a particularly desirable diversion.

At home, the student is expected to do activities of his or her choice with a family member for at least a half hour. Then, a family member documents their activities in the composition notebook included in the pack. But often they go beyond just documenting what they did with their children. In her first experience with sending the backpack home, for example, Suzy received notes from parents and students, letting her know when supplies were low or that game pieces were missing. Sometimes families described what they chose to play and enjoyed most. One time, a particularly lively family challenged the next family to create a shape they had made using the bag's tangram set. In the spirit of friendly competition, this challenge took off and lots of vigorous exchanges were recorded in the notebook.

Suzy reads through the notebook each morning when it is returned, occasionally using information to replenish supplies and make repairs. Often she adds a few lines to the entry when she wants to point out a connection to a previous entry, offer a challenge of her own, or ask a question of future users. She also rotates games and books each quarter to keep the activities fresh, adding family donations of card games and number activity books when they come in.

Suzy does not formally evaluate the math backpack experience, beyond noting when a student has taken his or her turn and recorded a notebook entry. She also jots down information that might support her Weekly-Update writing or report-card evaluations. For example, if a student is repeatedly using the backpack's tangrams or geoboards, she assumes an interest in geometry. This allows her to put together a richer composite of the student's development when reporting progress to his family.

For students who really enjoy taking the backpack home, Suzy has a system that allows those young mathematicians to have the bag more frequently: She rotates the pack regularly Monday through Thursday, but leaves Fridays open to whomever is quick enough to get his or her name on the sign-up calendar. Holidays and long weekends are the hottest times!

The math backpack is an effective way to make an academic connection between school and home in a non-threatening, entertaining way. As the backpack changes hands and students and their families share words, Suzy's class extends the influence of their community beyond classroom walls. The friendly competition and genuine learning opportunities that the backpack provides foster a better understanding of the environment the class works to sustain. And the rich dialogue it inspires in homes is priceless.

Closing Thoughts

The math backpack is just one example of how talk in classrooms can be extended to talk in homes. But it is also a powerful example of how working hard on building community in and out of school pays rich dividends when it comes to learning in the classroom.

In the next chapter, we'll take a close look at other examples of how combining social interaction with academics at the beginning of the year can create a dynamic curriculum in grades three to six.

Chapter 6

Academic Connections

*Setting the Stage for Deep Learning
Across the Curriculum*

"*Coming together is a beginning, keeping together
is progress, working together is success.*" ● *Henry Ford*

We hope that at this point you have many good ideas for
how to launch the school year in a way that fosters community and communication throughout the year. But schools
are first and foremost about learning. Once students make personal connections and develop a respectful rapport, what
next? For every grade level, curricular guides and mandates

are filled with both required content, standards which must be met, and practical activities. We've often felt overwhelmed and discouraged when we look at these guides—at the sheer number of requirements and possibilities.

In this last stretch of the book, we want to share some of our favorite early-year activities that build bridges between the academic and the social, across the curriculum. We begin by discussing service learning as a way to integrate curricular areas. From there, we move into individual curricular areas, suggesting activities to get you thinking about how to build bridges in your own classroom.

Making the Most of Service Learning

Service learning is an area of great interest in the upper-elementary grades. We've found that students really dive into helping others when they're given the option and encouraged. Service learning activities not only help students see that they can make a difference in their community, but they also give students a real reason to apply what they're learning in all subject areas. Here are a few examples.

● CONNECTING SERVICE LEARNING TO MATH

Five fifth-grade classes at State Street School in Brewer, Maine, conduct a food drive every fall. Students in each class keep a tally of how many items they have brought in and graph their bounty day to day. They also create bar graphs comparing the amount of items across classrooms.

● CONNECTING SERVICE LEARNING TO SCIENCE

Another class cleaned up the shallow slow stream behind their school, counting and weighing all the debris they removed. In the spring, these students studied the development of frogs, from eggs to tadpoles to four-legged creatures, in the clean stream.

Celebrating Make a Difference Day, a national event which happens in October, is a good way to introduce students to service learning. Different classes can identify one project to work on for part of that day—for example, picking up trash around the school, weeding the garden outside a town office, or reading to younger children. From there, students can write a brief report or share their experiences with other classes. In our experience, students often receive a thank you from the person or group they helped.

Looking at Individual Curricular Areas

Service learning helps students move beyond themselves by making a difference in and tying academics to the real world. However, you don't need to plan an extended service learning project to set the stage for deep learning across the curriculum. In the following sections, we'll take a look at activities and lessons in specific curricular areas that do double duty: build community and promote academic skills. Some of these ideas can be implemented quickly. Others will happen over time. But they all share one goal: helping students understand the value of learning while working with others.

Reading: Recommended Books

Jill Ostrow saves an area of her classroom for a "Recommended Books" display. During the first week of school, for homework, she asks each student to bring in a favorite book, think about why he or she likes the book, what kind of person might like the book, and pick a favorite passage to read aloud. She also chooses her own book and passage for the display, before school begins. From there, she and the students talk about their choices. For example, one year Jill brought in a picture book by Patricia Polacco, which she had read that summer, and explained to her students why she decided on it: "I know some of you haven't read a picture book in a

Service Learning Resources

The Web site www.servicelearning. org/resources_tools/ contains service-learning ideas and opportunities, including lessons for Earth Day projects and much more.

111

long time, but you should! We'll be looking at some great picture books this year. This one is about the Civil War and is called, *Pink and Say*." Jill explained to the class why the book was important to her, discussed the illustrations, and made connections to other books by Patricia Polacco. This book, and Jill's write-up of why it was one of her favorites, went onto the recommended books display table.

One of the students, Allen, took Jill's cue. He brought in a book by Stephen King and told the class, "I discovered Stephen King this summer and I love his stuff! Not all of you will like it, it's kind of gory, but if you like scary, gory stuff, this is the author for you." Allen then opened to his chosen passage—one that wasn't too gory—and read to the class.

As students present their books, the display grows over the first days and weeks of school. In the process, students get a sense of their classmates as readers. They also get an idea of authors they might like to read and authors who wouldn't interest them. For instance, Daniel, a child who was very interested in the Civil War, plucked *Pink and Say* right up to read. But Debra knew she'd never choose Stephen King after Allen read his passage. The book display changes throughout the year as students continue to recommend good books to their classmates.

While recommending books helps build community, it also helps students develop a crucial reading skill in the upper-elementary grades: discerning what books they can read and why certain books are appropriate for them and others aren't. Once students have "cracked the code" in reading, helping them make both just-right and challenging choices is a daunting task. The "Recommended Books" display helps them practice making wise choices and exposes them to fresh possibilities throughout the year.

Writing: Writing Strengths Chart

In Suzy Kaback's classroom, students are given opportunities to display their talents as often as possible. While they usually don't have trouble sharing their personal strengths on the All About Us bulletin board, or in an opening or closing moment (see Chapter 2), asking them to extol their academic strengths is another story. One way that Suzy makes it easier for them is with the writing strengths chart that students work on during the first weeks of school.

On a large piece of chart paper divided into two columns, Suzy writes the names of students in the class down the left-hand side. She labels the right-hand column "I'm skilled at …" From there, she asks each student to think of a writing strategy he or she feels comfortable using and offering to others. Students then write the strategy next to their names. Later, if students need help applying a particular strategy, they go to the class expert.

Many students can quickly name their strategy, but others need guidance. To help them, Suzy asks the class to brainstorm a list of "what good writers do." Behaviors students call out might include basic clean-up skills related to spelling, punctuation, and grammar. But often they offer less obvious behaviors such as thinking of titles, naming characters, choosing exciting verbs, coming up with topics, writing character descriptions, suggesting plot or setting details, and creating realistic dialogue.

As students begin filling in their writing strengths, surprises often emerge. For example, it's common for a student or two to assign himself a strategy that he *wishes* he handled well but, in reality, doesn't. However, when a classmate approaches him for expert help, rather than floundering, he rises to the challenge. Suzy had a student named Nate who wrote all of his stories' protagonists out of the most life-threatening situations with the same ending: "And then he woke up and found out it was all a

Sample Writing Strengths Chart

Writing Strengths

Who to see when you need feedback about your writing

Name	I'm skilled at...
Eric	Thinking of names for characters
Jill	Spell checking
Laura	Adding adjectives to describe scenes
Paul	Writing endings that make sense
Tim	Using realistic dialogue
Suzannah	Noticing places where a good verb is needed
Jolene	Rhyming, especially lyrics
Delaney	Figuring out where paragraphs go
Peter	Writing action scenes & sound effects
Patrick	Thinking of ideas to write about
Ella	Finding a way to begin a story with oomph!
Nick	Writing nonfiction
Marco	Illustrating scenes from writing
Meg	Turning facts into historical fiction
Kelsey	Adding graphics to nonfiction writing
Tessa	Punctuation
Ben	Describing the bad guys in a story
Mrs. Kaback	Making sure the writing flows

dream." Despite that, next to his name on the chart, Nate wrote: "I'm good at writing story endings."

Anticipating that she would be seeing a lot of "… it was all a dream" endings from kids who consulted Nate for ideas, Suzy was pleasantly surprised to discover that Nate had other tricks up his sleeve. When she asked him to step outside his own writing habits, he was able to offer suggestions that encouraged classmates to write with originality.

The writing strengths chart supports the group's growth as a community of writers throughout the school year, but it is particularly effective in September. The chart highlights the writing assets of Suzy's students, even if sometimes they have to stretch a bit to find those assets. By focusing collectively on what students can do well—at all the skills they *already* hold—Suzy sets a tone for collaboration and success. The language she uses makes a difference.

Social Studies: We, the Students

The United States Constitution is often discussed in the upper-elementary grades, as part of the American history curriculum. Often it is perceived as a dry document, rather than as a passionate, vital record of beliefs and goals. One way to bring our country's constitution to life is to have students write their own constitution for their class.

On the first day of school, Janet Nordfors calls her fourth graders to a class meeting to discuss their hopes and dreams. Her students sit in chairs in a circle, after practicing the best way to do that—calmly, directly, and without shoving or invading others' space. For over an hour, they discuss honestly the classroom they hope to create. Issues of respect, kindness, and caring are repeatedly brought up. Students often share personal experiences of when they've been treated well and when they haven't. Playground incidents always come up. It is amazing

Looking for fun, interactive ways to teach American history?

Try these books of fact-based read-aloud plays, written specifically for the upper-elementary grades, published by Scholastic Professional Books.

✔ *Revolutionary War* by Dallas Murphy

✔ *Civil War* by Timothy Nolan

✔ *Immigration* by Sarah J. Glasscock

✔ *Pioneers* by Dallas Murphy

We the people of the
United States, in
order to form a more
perfect union, estab-
lish justice, insure
domestic tranquility,
provide for the com-
mon defense, promote
the general welfare,
and secure the bless-
ings of liberty to our-
selves and our posteri-
ty, do ordain and
establish this
Constitution for the
United States of
America.

how deeply children can be hurt when they are
excluded from a game or called names by peers.

Disclosures like these help to develop a sense of
trust among students. After listing hopes and dreams
for their class, the students make a list of expectations
to correspond to their hopes and dreams, such as "a
peaceful classroom," "fair rules," "safety on the playground." After an hour they move on, to return to the
activity the next day.

The following day Janet takes out a copy of the preamble to the Constitution and reads it to the class. With
the students, she discusses what the words and phrases
mean. Next, they take their expectations from the day

Our Class Constitution

We the students of Mrs. Nordfors' class, in order to
form a more perfect classroom community, establish
expectations, insure peacefulness, provide for safety,
promote a learning environment, and secure the
blessings of a public education to ourselves and other
learners, do establish this Constitution of Caring for
our classroom.

We pledge to:
  I. Embrace our classroom values:
        Be Caring
        Be Respectful
        Be Trustworthy
        Be Responsible
        Be a Family
  II. Stay in our own space.
  III. Help each other.
  IV. Have a positive attitude and do our best.
  V. Have some fun.

Signed on the tenth day of September in the year 2003.

before and, together, write a paragraph that states them in a manner similar to the preamble. Then, they add a list of class rules. (See example on page 116.) After printing out an official version, Janet and the students all sign it. And it is then hung in the class for all to see.

Throughout the year, as the class studies American history in greater depth, students return to their own constitution as they consider the values underlying the American Constitution.

Math: Class Checkbooks

Inspiration often strikes when you're least expecting it. Suzy was reminded of this one evening in the checkout line at the grocery store. She took out her checkbook and began filling in the date, the name of the grocery store, and her signature, when suddenly—*Bingo!* She realized what a great math activity keeping checkbooks would be. The ins and outs of keeping track of a bank account is a real-life skill, and the idea of using real checkbooks to teach this skill was appealing. So Suzy started planning right away.

As the basis for the project, Suzy wanted to create a realistic currency exchange. She also wanted to find a link between the checkbooks and some of the community goals she had for the class. The result was the "Kaback National Bank." At the bank, each student opened an account and was given a checkbook for recording and spending the money they earned for positive individual and group behavior. The list of money-earning actions was compiled by Suzy and posted in the front of the class-room. Then on designated days, the students could spend their income at the class "market," where they would write checks to pay for their purchases. Suzy followed the steps below to launch and sustain the checkbook project:

1. First, she contacted her local bank and made arrangements for a guest speaker to talk with the class about the basics of checking account manage-ment. She asked for a set of checkbook registers

(enough for the whole class plus a few extras). The bank employee spoke with the students about how to manage a checking account and led them through sample exercises in depositing money, writing checks, and withdrawing from their balances. Suzy has found that bank personnel enjoy these class visits—and it's good publicity for the bank, too!

2. Second, Suzy designed math mini-lessons around checkbook skills to reinforce the guest speaker's lessons. Her mini-lessons focus on adding and subtracting decimals, understanding banking language (such as the terms "credit," "debit," "transfer," "balance," "fees," and "overdraft"), and explaining the basics of finance (e.g., money management, consumerism, saving, and spending).

3. Next, Suzy designed a regulation-size check to be used by the class. (Computer graphics are great resources for adding special touches to the class checks, and computer-savvy students can be especially helpful with this task.) Suzy photocopied enough checks for each student to begin with a set of ten to use with the registers given to them by the bank.

4. The checks needed protection, so Suzy laminated sheets of construction paper and cut them to make checkbook covers. She stapled checkbook registers and the set of ten checks inside the covers and distributed them to the class. Students wrote their names on a white label on the outside of the covers.

5. With their checkbooks assembled, the students were ready for the fun to begin. Behind the scenes, Suzy had been busy developing a list of positive behaviors she wanted to highlight in the classroom. Because it rewarded both individual and group achievement, she saw the checkbook project as a great beginning-of-the-year activity to

reinforce the kids' attitudes about teamwork. After making the list of desirable behaviors and their monetary values, Suzy posted it in a visible place in the classroom. The list included keeping desks neat, returning signed forms on time, having a perfect week of turning in homework, and remembering clothes for P.E. She also had frequent "unadvertised" specials, such as awarding a nickel to each person when the class transitioned from one class period to another particularly smoothly. Suzy felt that it was important to keep the list flexible and surprising in order to keep the students' interest in it high.

6. The Kaback National Bank was then open for business. When students accomplished one of the listed tasks, they earned the specified amount of money to deposit in their checkbooks. The students were responsible for keeping track of their deposits, and for the first two weeks Suzy collected their checkbooks every other day and left little sticky notes of encouragement. (This extra attention early on bought Suzy the students' confidence that she was watching their math more carefully than she really was.) After the first two weeks, she collected checkbooks on Fridays, or on an as-needed basis. She decided not to get into major record keeping because it would have been too much of a time drain. Instead, the class worked on the honor system and Suzy did spot checks. If a child looked like he had an unusual amount of money, or not as much as expected, Suzy might grab her calculator and check the balance. Or she might talk with a student about the honesty of his or her deposit and withdrawal recordings. Such conversations were rare events, though.

As the money-earning frenzy began, Suzy was deliberate in talking with students about the benefits and pitfalls of a checkbook system connected to behavior. (See list of reminders below.) She was careful to discuss the honor system that governed the project. Suzy told the class that if the activity produced too much anxiety, it would be abandoned.

7. Market Day was an important part of the checkbook project. This highlight happened each Friday afternoon when the class went to the class "market" to spend their income. Suzy would set up a table of goods, with each object assigned a price. Items for sale included books Suzy had purchased with bonus points from book club orders, fancy pens and pencils, bookmarks, erasers, small stuffed animals, and other miscellaneous things that teachers mysteriously accumulate. There were also less tangible items for sale, such as extra recess minutes, a whole-class video-watching period, a popcorn party, or an afternoon of playing games. These purchases were expensive and students often had to pool their money to afford one—which was, of course, part of the grand community-building plan. When kids used their individually-earned income to benefit the entire group, it reinforced a culture of teamwork and generosity.

8. Finally, Suzy wrote about the checkbook project in her class newsletter. She put extra emphasis on the fact that the activity was a community builder, and that discussion about the dangers of rewards was part of an integrated social studies lesson.

As she reflects on the checkbook project, Suzy realizes that it comes close to violating some of her teaching bottom lines. For example, as a rule she is not a big behaviorist; she prefers to work with her students to help them understand that a happy classroom is the best reward for good words and deeds. The checkbook idea definitely strays into the territory of material rewards, but Suzy tempers some of the potential negative effects in several ways. First, she is careful to list only positive behaviors as money-earners—those that all kids could achieve. Great scores on assignments, for example, are not worthy of cash. Also, kids cannot "lose" money for inappropriate actions. The focus is on what they do well, and any negative behavior is handled according to the regular rules of the class. Third, Suzy keeps a high-stakes feeling out of the checkbook project by emphasizing the benefits of teamwork. If the whole class returns their library books on time one week, each person earned a dime. If everyone brought their Weekly Reports back to school by Tuesday, the class earned fifteen cents.

These group incentives encourage students to remind each other of routine responsibilities. One year, a student started a Sunday-evening phone chain to remind everyone in the class to bring their signed field trip forms in by Monday. When the whole class showed up with the completed forms, everyone earned a quarter. This kind of cooperation is exactly the behavior Suzy hoped would grow from the checkbook project. By carefully but discreetly managing this activity, she can reinforce the rewards of community collaboration.

To Ensure Class Checkbook Success:

- *Maintain a positive tone.*
  Have students earn money for superior individual and group behavior.

- *Keep both the earned income and the cost of market items low.*
  (A week of turning in all homework on time should earn twenty-five cents; keeping a desk organized is worth a dime.) Save the big money-earners for tasks that can only be accomplished with help. (When the class as a whole has no overdue books at the library, each student earns a dollar for his checkbook.) One academic benefit of dealing with amounts less than a dollar is that kids get lots of practice with decimals!

(continued on the next page)

- *Revise the list frequently to keep interest high.*

- *Talk with your students about the effects of rewards.*
  This is a great opportunity for a social studies lesson. Be open about how attaching rewards to a behavior can make an otherwise pleasant task suddenly seem undesirable. Hold regular debriefings about the progress of the project. Let kids know that you'll bail out if the checkbooks are promoting negative actions, such as cheating in the record keeping or tattletaling.

- *Beware of assigning every deed a dollar amount.*
  Kids will start to ask if a behavior can be added to the list. Resist! Remember that the goal of the checkbooks is to build community, so choose money-earning behaviors discriminately.

- *Never take money away.*
  The potential for the checkbooks to become a major behavior manager is great. Imagine your class goes on a field trip to a museum and they behave atrociously. It might be tempting to wipe everybody's checkbook balance clean as a strong statement of your disappointment—but don't. Keep sacred the positive tone of the checkbooks.

- *Avoid overuse.*
  When students' enthusiasm for the checkbook project wanes—and it will—phase out the activity. Let students know that the checkbooks have a limited life span, maybe 10 weeks, and then you'll move on. By putting a time limit on the project from the start, students won't be surprised when it's time to pack up their checkbooks. To help ease the transition, encourage them to use the checkbooks for their own imaginative purposes at home or in school.

- *Wait at least a few weeks to introduce the checkbooks.*
  At the very beginning of the year, there should be a stretch where the idea of "good behavior for good behavior's sake" is clearly reinforced.

Science: My Tree

Good science is built on skillful observation. Scientists develop essential knowledge by learning to pay attention to the smallest details.

With that in mind, Jill Ostrow has her students go outside on the first day of school and choose a tree that they will observe all year. She provides them with tree journals that she creates by stapling together lined and blank paper. From there, they sketch their trees, look closely at the bark and leaves through magnifying glasses, and read guide books to try and identify them. Then, all students walk around to look at each tree, while the person who chose it gives a short introduction such as, "My name is Mary and this is my tree. It's a blue spruce and one thing I notice about it is that it is short, even shorter than I am! One thing I'm going to watch all year is whether it grows, and the rate of growth month by month if it does get bigger."

This is a simple activity that Jill adapts easily, depending on her goals for the class throughout the year. If the weather is good, students go outside each day and expand upon their writing about the tree. As Internet resources are discovered, students spend more time doing online research. Throughout the year, Jill returns to the tree journals and guidebooks. Students chart changes and hypothesize why they are occurring. This kind of investigation provides a springboard for studying climate, weather, and life cycles. And each student feels a personal connection to the tree he or she has chosen.

Concluding Thoughts

We hope these ideas get you thinking about ways to link the hard work of community building with the challenges of the curriculum. We've found our students blossom when they are able to combine their strengths as members of a community with learning throughout the curriculum. And activities like these, which can be extended throughout the year, are threads that tie students to each other.

Afterword

Inventing a Community

"Realize that change is not always a process of improvement.

Sometimes it is a process of invention. When Thomas Edison invented the light bulb, he didn't start by trying to improve the candle. He decided he wanted better light and went from there."

● *Wendy Kopp*

Writing this book has been exciting. Imagine having the opportunity to share with an interested audience all those great ideas you put into action throughout a school year! We hope it helps you think more about the choices you make to foster relationships and learning in your classrooms, and the reasons behind those choices. We believe that being able to answer the question "Why?" is one of the most important professional responsibilities a teacher has. With that in mind, we encourage you to look closely at what works in your classroom, as we have, and develop strong rationales for those practices. Use this book to help you support your theories in action.

But we also hope this book inspires you to invent,

and not just refine, what you already do. Sometimes the biggest and best ideas you discover won't fit with anything you've done before. In the moment of trying something wholly new, we hope you find yourself in a classroom community that has been transformed, at least in a small way.

We wanted to find a balance between *ways of thinking* about launching the school year and practical ideas for making it happen. We tried hard to avoid what Julie Wollman-Bonilla calls "succumbing to the highly seductive call of reductionism, making work in classrooms appear neat, easy and foolproof, if you just do it right." Beware of one-size-fits-all recommendations, even if they come from us! We recognize that classrooms are hotbeds of complexity with the individual needs of a group trumping any single approach to community building. We hope this book helps you honor what you do well, while supporting your interest in creating comfortable spaces where students question, learn, and grow. We wish you a happy beginning this fall and a safe, successful journey throughout the rest of the year.

Bibliography of Professional Resources

Allington, R., and Cunningham, P. *Schools That Work: Where All Children Read and Write*. New York: HarperCollins College Publishers, 1996.

Bany-Winters, L. *On Stage: Theater Games and Activities for Kids*. Chicago: Chicago Review Press, 1997.

Conklin, T. *Mystery Plays: 8 Plays for the Classroom*. New York: Scholastic, 1999.

Darling-Hammond, L. *The Right to Learn*. San Francisco: Jossey-Bass Publishers, 1997.

Denton, P., and Kriete, R. *The First Six Weeks of School*. Greenfield, MA: Northeast Foundation for Children, 2002.

Developmental Studies Center. *Ways We Want Our Class to Be*. Oakland, CA: Developmental Studies Center, 1996.

Erion, P. *Drama in the Classroom: Creative Activities for Teachers, Parents & Friends*. Fort Bragg, CA: Lost Coast Press, 1991.

Glasscock, Sarah J. *Read-Aloud Plays: Immigration*. New York: Scholastic: 1999.

Goodlad, J. *A Place Called School*. New York: McGraw-Hill Book Company, 1984.

Jensen, E. *Teaching with the Brain in Mind*. Alexandria, VA: Association for Supervision and Curriculum Development, 1998.

Kriete, R. *The Morning Meeting Book*. Greenfield, MA: Northeast Foundation for Children, 2002.

Kristo, J. "Getting to Know You, Getting to Know All About You." In *Whole Language Voices in Teacher Education*, ed. K. Whitmore and Y. Goodman. York, ME: Stenhouse, 1996.

MacDonald, M. R. *The Skit Book: 101 Skits from Kids*. North Haven, CT: Shoe String Press, 1990.

Meeks, L. and Heit, P. *Comprehensive School Health Education: Totally Awesome Strategies for Teaching Health.* Blacklick, OH: Meeks Heit Publishing Co, 1992.

Murphy, D. *Read-Aloud Plays: Pioneers.* New York: Scholastic, 1999.

Murphy, D. *Read-Aloud Plays: Revolutionary War.* New York: Scholastic, 2000.

Nelsen, J., Lott, L., and Glenn, S. *Positive Discipline in the Classroom.* Roseville, CA: Prima Publishing, 2000.

Nolan, T. *Read-Aloud Plays: Civil War.* New York: Scholastic, 1999.

Osterman, K. (2000). "Students' Need for Belonging in the School Community." *Review of Educational Research* 703:323-367.

Pugliano-Martin, C. *Read-Aloud Plays: Tall Tales.* New York: Scholastic, 2000.

Rooyackers, P., and Bowman-Hurd, C. *101 Drama Games for Children: Fun and Learning with Acting and Make-Believe.* Alameda, CA: Hunter House, 1997.

Styles, D. *Class Meetings: Building Leadership, Problem Solving and Decision Making Skills in a Respectful Classroom.* Portland, ME: Pembroke/Stenhouse, 2001.

Wilson, J., and Wing, L. *Thinking for Themselves: Developing Strategies for Reflective Learning.* Melbourne: Eleanor Curtain Publishers, 1993.

Wollman-Bonilla, J. (2002). "Does Anybody Really Care? Research and Its Impact on Practice." *Research in the Teaching of English* 311-326.

Wright, E. *Loving Discipline A-Z.* San Francisco: Teaching From the Heart, 1996.

Yero, J.(2002). "That Elusive Spark." *Education Week* 21, 37:34 + 37.

Bibliography of Literature

Agee, J. *Go Hang a Salami! I'm a Lasagna Hog! And Other Palindromes*. New York: Farrar Straus & Giroux, 1992.

Avi. *Poppy*. New York: Orchard, 1995.

Byars, B. *Bingo Brown and the Language of Love*. New York: Puffin, 1991.

Curtis, C.P. *The Watsons Go to Birmingham*. New York: Bantam Books, 1997.

Curtis, C.P. *Bud, Not Buddy*. New York: Yearling Books, 2000.

Declements, B. *Nothing's Fair in Fifth Grade*. New York: Puffin, 1990.

Fitzgerald, J.D. *The Great Brain*. New York: Yearling Books, 1972.

Fleischman, P. *A Joyful Noise: Poems for Two Voices*. New York: Harper & Row, 1988.

Fleischman, P. *I Am Phoenix: Poems for Two Voices*. New York: Harper & Row, 1989.

King, S. *Pet Sematary*. New York: New American Library, 1984.

Lasky, K. *The Librarian Who Measured the Earth*. Boston: Little, Brown and Co., 1994.

Lebowitz, F. http://www.quotationpage.com/quotes/Fran_Lebowitz/11,2002.

Levy, E. *My Life as a Fifth Grade Comedian*. New York: HarperTrophy, 1998.

Milne, A. A. *Pooh's Little Instruction Book*. New York: Dutton Books, 1995.

Parks, B. *The Best School Year Ever*. New York: HarperTrophy, 1997.

Peck, R. *Soup*. New York: Random House, 1982.

Polacco, P. *Pink and Say*. New York: Philomel Books, 1994.

Schwartz, D. *G is for Googol*. Berkeley, CA: Tricycle Press, 1998.

Scieszka, J. *Math Curse*. New York: Viking, 1995.

Terban, M. *To Hot to Hoot: Funny Palindrome Riddles*. Boston: Houghton Mifflin Co., 1985.

Tilly, J. *Ant: The Definitive Guide*. Sebastopol, CA: O'Reilly, 2002.

White, E. B. *Charlotte's Web*. New York: Harper & Row, 1952.